WESTCOUNTRY ALES

WESTCOUNTRY ALES

ALES

AN A–Z OF
BEER AND BREWING
IN DEVON AND CORNWALL

Adrian Tierney-Jones

HALSGROVE

First published in Great Britain in 2002

British Library Cataloguing-in-Publication Data
A CIP record for this title is available from the British Library

ISBN 1 84114 204 2

HALSGROVE

Halsgrove House
Lower Moor Way
Tiverton, Devon EX16 6SS
Tel: 01884 243242
Fax: 01884 243325
email: sales@halsgrove.com
website: www.halsgrove.com

Printed and bound in Great Britain by Bookcraft (Bath) Ltd, Midsomer Norton

Contents

Acknowledgements 6

Introduction 7

A *is for* ale, animals (and Andrews)... 11

B *is for* boys, beer and birds (of prey)... 17

C *is for* CAMRA, country brews (and cheers!)... 37

D *is for* drinks in the Doghouse... 46

E *is for* Exe and the Exmoor effect... 53

F *is for* flavour, firkins and Fizgigs... 57

G *is for* glug, glass and gravity... 59

H *is for* hops, health and hauntings... 61

I *is for* inn, IPA (and imbibe)... 66

J *is for* jugs and jollyboats... 69

K *is for* keg, Keltek and Kripple Dick!... 71

L *is for* local, lager and last orders... 75

M *is for* malt, mild and milk stout... 80

N *is for* a noggin of nitro-keg... 85

O *is for* organic, otters and others... 89

P *is for* pub and a pint of porter... 99

R *is for* real ale and a really thirsty pig!... 109

S *is for* several superb local breweries... 115

T *is for* taste, tavern and Tally Ho... 135

V *is for* vintage and a very spooky ale... 143

W *is for* white, winter and wheal ale... 145

X *is for* XXXX-stra strong... 150

Y *is for* yeast and a yard of ale... 151

Z *is for* zzz... 152

Twelve of the Best – 153
 Some of the author's favourite Westcountry pubs

Bibliography 159

Dedication

To Jane – for everything

Acknowledgements

The first people I want to thank are the brewers at all the Devon and Cornwall breweries I visited or spoke to, who put up with me turning up and asking silly questions, especially when they were brewing. I would also like to thank them for their generosity in providing me with images and tasting samples for the book.

Many other people have helped me as well, including: Colin Heapy, without whose collection of Westcountry brewers' memorabilia I would have been lost; Adrian Newman at Exmoor Ales for casting an eye over the brewing entries; Brian Gates at Tuckers Maltings for permission to lift information from his excellent *Tuckers Maltings 1900–2000: History in the Making*; Westcountry CAMRA stalwarts Philip Roberts, Rod Davies, Ian Packenham (very helpful on Thompson's) and Steve Willmott; Exe Valley's Guy Sheppard; Ken Smith from the Brewery History Society who uncovered a wealth of pictures and information about Norman & Pring; John Preston at St Austell for his help with the brewery's history and permission to use pictures of the brewery; Rupert Ponsonby with his help on hops; plus anyone else whom I have forgotten to mention. Finally thanks also go to Halsgrove's Debbie Coxon who helped to get the book published.

As for pictures, they come from a variety of sources, including my own collection, the Brewery History Society, Tuckers Maltings, Colin Heapy, Young's Brewery and Cotleigh Brewery.

Introduction

I have spent the last year visiting the breweries of Devon and Cornwall, talking with the brewers and, of course, tasting their real ales. As many friends have put it: 'nice work!' People unfamiliar with the West Country might automatically think of cider when they consider the drink of Devon and Cornwall, but in fact these two counties have a long and proud history of brewing beer. Redruth, Exeter, St Austell, Plymouth and Tiverton are just a few of the towns and cities where major brewing operations have thrived at one time or another. Wander through the villages and towns of the West and names such as 'The Old Malthouse', 'The Brewhouse' and Brewery Road also testify to this shared past.

The people I have visited this year are proud inheritors of this great tradition. They are part of a vibrant network of Westcountry breweries producing real ale. Some are so small that they only produce a few casks of beer per brewing session; others are large commercial operations. Above them all towers St Austell, Cornwall's last surviving regional brewer, still producing wonderful beers two centuries on, running the gamut from a traditional dry-hopped bitter to an exotic wheat-beer style, flavoured with spices and vanilla. St Austell stands as solid as a rock on a historical site, where brewing has gone on for decades.

Some of these breweries are not so easy to find. Some, such as Otter and Exe Valley, lie hidden down deep lanes in converted farms and barns. Some intriguing small operations quietly work away at the back of a pub – the Blue Anchor and the Wheal Ale Brewery spring to mind. On the other hand, breweries such as the Ring O' Bells and Blackawton stand bold and brash on industrial units close to key roads so that they can get their beers out to Westcountry drinkers all the more quickly. Maybe not so quaint but it is certainly pragmatic – and today's brewers need barrel-loads of that, along with more than a pinch of common-sense and commercial sensibility to survive.

So what kind of beers are these brewers producing? While the Midlands own their milds, and London boasts its generously hopped and fruity ales such as Young's Special, there seems no single beer style around today which we can call Westcountry. Once upon a time the palate of the West (as far as beer was concerned) was supposed to be sweet – or so I'm told by those with long memories. Some of today's Westcountry beers still retain a slight whisper of sweetness in the finish but probably nothing like it used to be. After the travails of the Second World War, when barley and hops were in short supply, brewers wanted to make their beers consistent and many were indeed sweeter, probably because of the post-war liking for such flavours. However if there is a dominant trend in the twenty-first century, then it is for fruity and hoppy beers (but less bitter than their northern cousins).

This is a wonderfully exciting time for beer in the West Country. Today's brewers are creating tasty and flavoursome beers, and recreating classic beers from the past, making them even better than before. There is much experimentation with hops going on, while the concept of 'going organic' interests quite a few brewers. It could be said that the West's micro-breweries have a willingness to take chances, to experiment and celebrate the culture of brewing; maybe a lot more than some of their micro-cousins elsewhere in England, suggested one Cornish brewer I spoke to. And what beers they all make: everyday session bitters with fresh hoppy noses and a lingering bitterness; fruity and hoppy best bitters; malty milds; unusual beers flavoured with honey, fruit and, in the odd case, cloves and coriander; wheat beers; real lagers; barley wines; Christmas beers, vintage ales; historical recreations, and the odd porter and stout. One thing I discovered was that dark beers are not made as much as I would like them to be. But that is a small gripe when we have the likes of Skinner's Mild Oatmeal Stout, Sutton's Madiba Stout, Organic Brewhouse's Black Rock Stout or O'Hanlon's Port Stout.

There are also grain hopper-loads of excellent pubs in the West Country where you can find (and drink) pints of these great beers. It is cheering (for a real ale drinker) to discover that a great many are free houses while others belong to breweries (mainly St Austell). Of course a sizeable amount are still owned by pub companies, the majority of whom rightly or wrongly have a reputation for restricting the selection of real ales their managers can buy. For this reason, it is not always easy to taste the best of the West in local pubs. All too often, most of the real ales, though superbly kept, come from outside the area and some drinkers could spend their lives never tasting the tongue-tingling likes of the Organic Brewhouse or Jollyboat. But a tiny amount of detection work will usually turn up the perfect pub to fit your taste – a lively place of social conviviality or a quiet corner in which to sip and watch the world go by. And drink local beers, of course.

I hope you enjoy this 'session' with Westcountry ales as much as I've enjoyed researching and writing it. Above all I hope it encourages you to seek out and savour the wonderful ales of Devon and Cornwall, or who knows maybe even start a brewery yourself.

Cheers

Adrian Tierney-Jones

Note: Where possible, I have listed the strength of every beer mentioned. The strength of the majority of the beers uses the Alcohol By Volume measurement scale (ABV). However, some now-defunct beers are measured by their Original Gravity (OG), which was the scale used when these breweries were working. Please see relevant entries for ABV and Original Gravity.

A *is for*
ale, animals (and Andrews)...

ABV

When you order a beer take a look at the label halfway up the pump. You will see the beer's name and a number followed by the letters ABV, as in Devon Dawn ABV 4.5%. This is the standard scale of alcoholic strength, otherwise known as alcohol by volume; it tells you what percentage of alcohol there is in your finished beer and hence how strong it will be. (See **Original Gravity.**)

Spot the ABV: Exe Valley Bitter and a hand-written handpump for Dob's Best Bitter

Ale

The word 'ale' is derived from the Anglo-Saxon 'ealu'. Ale was originally a malted alcoholic drink which used herbs and spices to clarify, season or preserve it. Up until the sixteenth century when hops were introduced into England (along with turkey, carp, pickerel and beer, according to one anonymous rhyme), the words beer and ale were interchangeable. Afterwards, beer came to mean the hopped variant. In the 1570s, ale was compared unfavourably with beer: 'thick and fulsome and not popular except with a few'. In the far west, Cornish ale was described as 'looking white and thick as if pigs had wrestled in

Hail the ale: label for Norman and Pring's Nap Ale

11

it'. Nowadays ale survives as an all-purpose word for beer, as in 'A pint of ale, landlord'. We also talk about variations such as mild ale, pale ale and India Pale Ale. (See **Beer**.)

Ale Bush

In the Middle Ages, this was the customary sign for an inn – a clump of ivy and vine leaves was placed on a pole outside.

Ale Conner

Even though he's not called an ale conner, Teignworthy Brewery worker and Newton Abbot's port reeve Derek Newland does a similar job when he puts on his robes to test the town's beers in June. Here, he's seen judging beer at the Tuckers Maltings' festival

This was a lucky individual appointed by the authorities to go and taste all the beers in the locality to check they were fit for consumption and that the prices were fair. It began in the Middle Ages and there were still four ale conners engaged by the City of London after the Second World War. The practice was recently revived with four ale conners being appointed once more to the City of London. Newton Abbot Council still has an official ale-taster who makes his appearance at the annual Tuckers Maltings' festival held in the town. Newton Abbot also hosts the Ancient Ceremony of Ale Tasting in June, with a procession of town worthies in full ceremonial fig visiting all 16 pubs within the ancient borough's boundaries. This tradition apparently dates back to medieval times when the local bigwig would get his man on the ground to make sure that all the beer sold to the peasants was of sufficient quality. Ashburton also has a similar ceremony with ale-tasters making a day-long round of the town's pubs in July.

Ales of Scilly   St Mary's, Isles of Scilly

Mark Praeger was a teacher for twenty-five years. For fourteen of those years, he was deputy headmaster at a primary school on the islands. He was also an occasional home-brewer, a hobby which started when,as a a twelve-year-old schoolboy, he was sent home with a nature-based project. While the other pupils looked to flowers and plants for inspiration, Mark thought yeast might make a good subject and brewed some beer. It went down well all round, and so began a lifelong hobby which stood him in good stead when he quit teaching in 2001, and set up a 2.5-barrel brewery in a two-storey barn at Higher Trenoweth on the island of St Mary's.

The Isles of Scilly have never been noted for their real ale. As Mark says, 'Real ale didn't really exist here until the last couple of years. It was all keg with a bit of St Austell. So something had to be done about it.' He researched the nuts and bolts of brewing, using the internet and making many trips to the mainland. Equipment and raw materials were bought (malt from Tuckers Maltings, hops from Charles Farham in Herefordshire); recipes were tested, and by

September 2001 he was selling his beer. The first sample out of the fermenting vessels was a golden-coloured session beer, Maiden Voyage, a name that seemed appropriate for a first launch as Mark enjoys sailing in his spare time. The second beer was Scuppered, a chestnut-brown coloured premium ale. It is a beer to be taken seriously. Mark recalls:

I had a chap come over from a Cornish pub with a couple of mates who were down for the weekend. They tasted Scuppered and liked it so much that they visited the brewery and we had a couple of drinks. I later heard that one of them had nine pints of it in the pub and had to be wheelbarrowed back to the guest-house.

These bibulous visitors will be glad to hear that there are other beers planned, plus some bottling so that visitors can take a taste of the Isles of Scilly home with them.

Brewing on the Scilly Isles presents something of a challenge. During the winter Mark brews once a week, which presents him with eight to nine casks, but during the busy summer he hopes to be making beer three times a week. The bulk of his sales are obviously on the island as freight costs make exporting them prohibitively expensive. However, some are sent to mainland wholesalers for beer festivals and the like. Tourist trade is inevitably very important but what is also cheering is that the beers are popular with the locals. Mark says:

I was speaking to someone about it, and they told me they were proud to have a local brewery, which surprised me as I had always just thought of it as a business. There was a sort of civic pride in it.

Beers: Maiden Voyage (4%); Three Sheets (4.1%); Scuppered (4.6%).
Star Beer: Scuppered (4.6%) – Single varietal hop beer which uses the tangy and bitter Challenger hop, giving a clean flavour with hints of lemon. On the palate it starts with a hint of chocolate and nuttiness courtesy of the malt, before a subtle fruitiness takes over, followed by a long, dry and bitter finish with traces of maltiness.
Recommended outlets: The Scillonian Club, St Mary's; the Mermaid, St Mary's.

Animals

Horses used to pull drays and could be led into their village local for a quick half of mild and bitter. Cats caught rats and mice in breweries' grain stores, and coachloads of tourists would stop at Jamaica Inn near Bodmin to see the parrot. The Blisland Inn, near Bodmin, has a large

Pulling power: Cotleigh Brewery's dray and horses; bringing back a long lost tradition

*Animal magic:
Ring O' Bells' Porker's Pride; Sutton Brewery's Pandamonium (below)*

green iguana in the corner of its family room. He is called Dino and gets his own fan mail. There is a pot-bellied pig and dwarf pony at Devon brewers O'Hanlon's, and the Ring O' Bells brewery in Cornwall also had a pot-bellied pig for its mascot (sadly now deceased), while on the Devon-Somerset border Cotleigh Brewery has close links with the Hawk and Owl Trust – they also have a vintage dray which is pulled by three shire-horses for deliveries in local pubs. However, the main use of animals in the beer world today has to be the names and pictures which adorn pub clips and beer bottle labels. Cotleigh has a whole range of bird-orientated names, while its Wiveliscombe neighbours Exmoor Ales go for the four-legged variant with beers such as Beast, Hound Dog and Stag. Let us not forget Otter Brewery whose light-hearted posters feature those cuddly river-bank dwellers enjoying all sorts of liquid delights including a yard of ale. Over the border in Cornwall, one of the county's newest breweries looks to dogs for its inspiration. Doghouse Brewery is, yes, situated in a boarding kennels, and produces beers such as Wet Nose, Biter and Bow Wow. Some of the brewery's publican customers can actually request a beer named after their pub dog. This comes with a specially produced pubclip featuring the mutt in question. Meanwhile, Wheal Ale brews a strong ale called Speckled Parrot. You cannot teach an old dog tricks, but you can get it to inspire you with a beer name.

Arctic Ales

This is a long-forgotten style of strong ale which first made its appearance in 1852, when Burton brewers Allsopp were commissioned by the authorities to provide a special beer for an Arctic expedition in search of the missing explorer Franklin. The ale was such a success that it was taken on other expeditions to the Polar regions. Ind Coope's Arctic Ale travelled with the British North Greenland expedition in 1952, an event which formed part of an advertising campaign. The Arctic Ale style was described as being less sweet than a barley wine and 'as mellow as old Burgundy and nourishing as beefsteak'. It vanished from view in the 1960s, but Teignworthy Brewery recently revived it with Edwin Tucker's Celebrated Arctic Ale.

Star Beer: Edwin Tucker's Celebrated Arctic Ale (9%) – A delicious dark ale with a rich malty nose. On the palate it has rich malt and fruit, with a powerful hoppiness and dryness lingering in the long finish. (See **Teignworthy**.)

Edwin Tucker's Celebrated Arctic Ale

Arnold & Hancock's   Wiveliscombe, Somerset

Any real ale drinker approaching Wiveliscombe on the Taunton road will have spotted the imposing brewery tower on Golden Hill, where Exmoor Ales' beers are brewed. However, until Exmoor and Cotleigh brought brewing back to the town, this Victorian tower was the sole sad reminder of the demise of one of the West Country's better-known brewers, Hancock's which later became Arnold & Hancock. The Hancocks were a local farming family and their fourth son William began brewing in 1806. With plenty of trade from thirsty local farm labourers and woollen workers, the business was successful and by 1842 William Hancock had six tied houses in Wiveliscombe. With the death of the brewery's founder the business passed to his son, William Hancock the Younger, who continued the good work. By the 1850s Hancock's were a major power in the county and a couple of decades later they were seen as the largest brewery in the West of England. However, 1927 saw the firm link up with SW Arnold & Sons of Rowbarton, Taunton, with brewing taking place in both locations and Wiveliscombe hosting the malting. The next, and sadly, final development came in the 1950s when Arnold & Hancock's became a subsidiary of Usher's of Wiltshire. 'Rationalisation' meant that brewing ceased in

The imposing brewery tower of Arnold & Hancock, a brewery which once dominated parts of the West Country

1959, and a year later a major part of local history went under the hammer. The plant and machinery were sold off and the premises disposed of, eventually becoming a chicken processing factory. (See **Cotleigh Brewery, Exmoor Ales.**)

Aroma

The first stage in beer tasting. For serious tastings some recommend a large red wine glass which allows the drinker to swirl the beer in order for the aromas to emerge. Depending on the beer, there will be aromas of malt (grainy, biscuity, nutty, bready, toasty), and hop (fruity, resiny, peppery, perfumey, aromatic, herbal), with an estery fruitiness (bananas, tropical fruit, peach) coming through on stronger beers. On dark beers you should recognise roast barley, chocolate and coffee bean aromas, followed by vinous fruit and a subtle underpinning of hoppiness. On barley wines, aromas include dried fruit, Christmas cake and maltiness. As the beer warms up, more and more aromas are released. (See **Hops, Tasting.**)

Aroma Hops

If all the hops for a brew were added at the start of the process most would escape up the chimney, so hops are added throughout, with certain hops being used for their aroma quality. These are usually hops with a low alpha acid quality and therefore not so bitter. The other name for them is late hops. (See **Hops.**)

Axe Vale Brewery Best Bitter: a good singing beer

Axe Vale Brewery   Colyton, Devon

In 1983 sales agent and metallurgy consultant Harry Kingsbury gave up his day job to start a small brewery with his wife. Three beers were produced, Best Bitter (OG 1040), Battleaxe (OG 1053) and Conqueror (OG 1066, naturally). 'This should be a good singing beer,' said Harry at the time, but there was more crying than singing three years later when the brewery closed.

Axminster Brewery: began brewing in 1988 and stopped a year later

Axminster Brewery   Fordwater, Axminster, Devon

Axminster started brewing in 1988 with a ten-barrel kit from the Hardington Brewery in Somerset. There were three regular beers: Axminster Bitter (OG 1036), the well-hopped and fruity Hardington Bitter (OG 1037) and the full-bodied Somerset Special (OG 1043). There was also a strong dark beer brewed for bank holidays called Horrors (OG 1050-55). Brewing lasted less than a year, with the equipment being sold on to another Hardington brewery, totally unconnected with the previous Hardington.

B *is for*
boys, beer and birds (of prey)...

Barley

Cereal crop which produces grain in the same way as a tree will produce berries, fruit or nuts. When the grain is part germinated and kilned it produces malted barley which is used in the first step in brewing. Roast barley is kilned but unmalted barley. (See **Brewing, Malt.**)

Barley Wine

...or Stingo, or Wee Heavy, as it is been called in other parts of the UK. For a start it is nothing to do with wine and all to do with beer. Like its close relations, old ales and winter warmers, it is a beer to be sipped and savoured. A coat of many colours is worn: dark, ruby-red, chestnut-brown or even golden. Whatever the hue, it is a full-bodied, rich-tasting and fruity beer to be sipped with great relish, preferably in front of a roaring log fire while the winter weather does its worst outside. With an ABV rising from 7% onwards it is definitely not something you swig in pints. Well you can, but beware: it was called a sitting down beer because there was less distance to fall. For this reason, most barley wines are sold in tiny bottles called nips. The name 'barley wine' is generally reckoned to have emerged at the turn of the twentieth century, but no one knows why. Maybe brewers wanted some of the social cachet of wine rubbing off on to their stronger products. Or maybe it was an attempt to push beer upmarket; during the later years of the Victorian age, Bartlett & Co. in Dartmouth called their beers the 'Barley Wine of the English Rhine'.

The long maturation in cask is barley wine's only real connection with wine-making. Today's barley wines are for the most part brewed earlier in the year and left to grow and develop their rich, complex tastes. Whatever the name's origins, the actual style of barley wine has been around as long as beer. In the days before refrigeration, summer-brewed beers could easily turn to vinegar so strong ales brewed in spring were indispensable as their alcoholic strength helped preservation. They were also useful for blending with weaker beers. At one stage nearly all

Where beer begins: a field of barley

A beer for bad weather: Keltek Brewery's barley wine: ironically enough, Kripple Dick was also the name of a St Austell barley wine

brewers made barley wine, with favourites in the West Country including St Austell's Smuggler's Strong Ale (7.8%), now discontinued. They also made a Kripple Dick as well. Sadly, there are only a few Westcountry barley wine style beers today with Teignworthy and Keltek leading the field. Audit Ales were also barley wines produced at the older universities, especially for the day of audit.

Star Beer: Kripple Dick (8.5%) – Very dark with ruby highlights, this kicks off with an emphatic malty nose, majoring on chocolate malt, with added dimension coming in from hints of Marmite, stewed fruit, cereal and Weetabix in warm milk. It is a light mouthfeel despite the strength, with sweetish maltiness balanced by a mid-palate fruitiness leading to a lingering bitter-sweet and fruity finish. There is also a whisper of cereal malt in the finish. Available in bottle and occasional draught.

Barrel

This is the layperson's term for a nine-gallon cask of beer, while those in the trade talk of a firkin. In the brewery a barrel is 36 gallons and a measure of the brew-length of a brewery. For instance, the Beer Engine is a three-barrel brewery: this means that it can brew 108 gallons in one go. St Austell, on the other hand, can handle 150 barrels at once.

Above: Inside the Beer Engine, a three-barrel brewery
Above right: Mervyn Westaway checks the mash tun at St Austell, which can produce 150 barrels in one go

Barron Brewery   Silverton, Devon

See Exe Valley Brewery.

Barnstaple Brewery   Barnstaple, Devon

Established at the Taw Vale Brewery, brewing began in 1851, but Arnold Perrett bought the business in 1895. It was then sold to Starkey, Knight & Ford in 1897, and closed in 1900. Several other breweries operated in the town between 1898 and 1930, but it was not until 1996 that brewing returned to Barnstaple with Barum Brewery. (See **Barum Brewery.**)

Bartlett & Co.   Dartmouth, Devon

South Devon brewery which started trading at Warfleet Mills in the middle of the nineteenth century. After a royal visit, Queen Victoria publicly noted the similarity of the Dart Valley to the Rhine Valley, and the brewery capitalised on this with a trademark slogan 'The barley wine of the English Rhine'. In the 1880s, owner Jasper Bartlett proclaimed Warfleet Pale Ales as 'the finest beer in Britain'. Advertising gimmicks notwithstanding, the brewery was taken over by Exeter's Heavitree in 1927 and brewing ceased a couple of years later.

Bartlett's Warfleet Brewery at Dartmouth in 1985, nearly 60 years after brewing stopped

Barum Brewery   Barnstaple, Devon

One of Barum's biggest fans is a short, portly chap with a monocle. Everywhere you see Barum's fine beers, you will also find this chap. Lord Basil is the face of Barum, a slightly, down-at-heel, Falstaffian cartoon character who appears on the front of every Barum pumpclip or bottle label, doing daft things. Created by a Beano cartoonist, he gives an air of playfulness and comic-book roguishness to Barum's image. This sense of fun is compounded by the brewery's slogan 'Beer's not just for breakfast anymore'. These are beers created by people who like beer and the joy it brings to drinkers. So it seems appropriate that you can find this five-barrel brewer at the back of a pub, the Reform Inn in Pilton, which has long been part of Barnstaple.

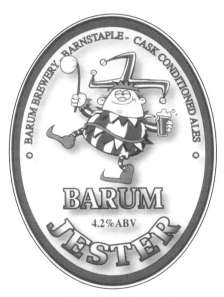

A sense of fun: Barum Brewery's Jester

Barum was set up in 1996 by local lad Tim Webster, who had spent the preceding fourteen years working for a computer company. It was a good job with all the associated benefits. However, he wanted to be his own boss. One day, while chatting with the then landlord of his local, the Reform Inn, he mused about starting up a brewery. He was not new to brewing, but he wanted the experience to be trouble-free this time. Tim once brewed beer at his monastery school but was expelled

The Thatched Barn Inn, Croyde where Barum's Longboat can be enjoyed, in between surfing sessions on the nearby beach

by the monks for various misdemeanours. There was also a small matter of the home-made explosives which resulted in him blowing off part of one of his fingers. The small brewery would be a part-time hobby at first, with Tim making beer at weekends and evenings. Brewing took place at the Reform, which was very handy as the beers could be sold there. Kit was sourced from the short-lived Combe Brewery in nearby Ilfracombe and a lean-to built at the back of the pub.

The first beers rolled out in the autumn of 1996, with Tim being helped by Brian Broughton, latterly of Combe. By July 1997, Tim took the big step and started brewing full-time. 'It was a bit of a leap of faith,' he says, 'and I went from well-paid executive to poor brewer.' The first beer to roll out of the fermenting vessels was Barum Original, a well-rounded best bitter. By the end of 1998, Brian had left to set up Clearwater in Torrington, but Barum was going great guns and had become a five-barrel operation, brewing four times a week. Demand has continued but space is limited at the Reform. To deal with this not-unwelcome problem, June 2001 saw the opening of Barum's second brewery, a 2.5-barrel brewplant at the back of The Castle Inn in George Nympton, near South Molton.

Over the years, Barum has produced over a dozen different beers. Like every other brewery it has its regulars. XTC is a tawny-coloured session bitter, with Challenger hops providing a sharp and clean bitterness, and Goldings the fruity nose. The refreshing Longboat is brewed especially for the Thatched Barn Inn at Croyde, while Original is a well-balanced best bitter with bite, thanks to the addition of roasted malt. Stronger beers include Breakfast, Challenger and the fruity, well-hopped strong ale Barnstablasta which comes out in the cold months. This was Champion beer at the 2001 Exeter and East Devon CAMRA Winter Beer Festival. Barum has also produced a lager, Barumburg. 'We did it because there are very few British breweries who do lager,' says Tim. 'We don't do it that often, but at least it is something different. What I look for in beers is individuality.' A bit like Lord Basil.

Beers: XTC (3.7%); Longboat (3.8%); Original (4.4%); Breakfast (5%); Challenger (5.6%); Barnstablasta (6.6%). Occasional: Barumburg (4.6%); BSE (3.7%); Dark Star (4.8%); Gold (4%); Liquid Lunch (4.6%); Technical Hitch (5.3%); Bottles: Original; Breakfast; Challenger; Barnstablasta, all bottle-conditioned.

Star Beer: Breakfast (5%) – This dark gold beer is stronger than it seems. There is plenty of citrus fruit on the nose and the palate, which is balanced by toasty, biscuity malt, plus the bite of dark malt. The finish is dry, bitter, lasting and full of hop fruitiness and some malt plus a subtle trace of sweetness.

The Reform Inn, Pilton, Barnstaple, home to a good pub and Barum Brewery round the back

Recommended outlets: The Reform Inn, Pilton, Barnstaple; The Castle Inn, George Nympton.

Bate's Brewery   Bovey Tracey, Devon

Founded in 1983 on an industrial estate by former builder Ron Bate. 'I got out of the business as I was fed up with the competition,' he said at the time. 'There's too many builders and not enough work.' It was a ten-barrel plant and the first beer to be brewed was the light-coloured Bate's Bitter (OG 1045). Sadly, brewing ended in 1986 when Ron Bate died.

Bedford Brewery   Plymouth

Brewing started in 1900 in the Mutley district in Plymouth, but the business was bought by Burton-on-Trent's Allsopp's in 1919 and merged with another Plymouth concern, Victoria Brewery. The operation was called the New Victoria Brewery and continued until the 1950s. (See **Victoria Brewery**.)

Beer

The word 'beer' is apparently derived from the Anglo-Saxon word 'beor' and was interchangeable with ale until the appearance of hops in England in the sixteenth century. Afterwards beer meant a fermented malt liquor which had been hopped and hence went into popular day-to-day use.

The Beer Engine Brewery   Newton St Cyres, Devon

In the early-1980s Yorkshireman Peter Hawksley was teaching social sciences at Exeter. He enjoyed good beer, but there was little of it in the area as Whitbread and Courage dominated the pubs. So, instead of crying into his pint, he decided to do something about it by setting up the Beer Engine brew-pub at Newton St Cyres, halfway between Exeter and Crediton. At the time it was called the Barn Owl. Prior to that it had a history dating to the nineteenth century when it started as an old railway pub for the then thriving station. Its original name was the Railway and had also been called the Iron Horse. Peter Hawksley toyed with the idea of reintroducing the Iron Horse, but he plumped for the Beer Engine. 'We started off with Rail Ale and Piston Ale,' he recalls, 'and they remain our two main beers today, even though they have been slightly modified over the years.'

A sign of good beer: The Beer Engine

The Beer Engine is a cosy and comfortable place to sample the brewery's ales. The interior is U-shaped with a long bar in the middle. There is a dining area at the far end, with plenty of dark wood, dried hops hanging up, and old pictures and engravings on the wall. The ceiling is traced with exposed beams and there are lots of little nooks

Above: *Rail ale at the Beer Engine*
Above right: *The Beer Engine, which has gone through several name changes*

and crannies. The walls are painted a soft terracotta which gives it all a warm feeling. It is a very friendly place with landlord Peter doing the chef's work, and his wife Jill taking the mealtime orders. Long-time barman Trevor pulls pints, when he is not joint Master of the local Stoke Hill Beagles. The three-barrel brewery is downstairs and it is the same kit they have had for nineteen years. Ian Sharp is the head brewer, but Peter decides what beers are going to be brewed and he always tries to help out with the mash. Hops used are Challenger, Goldings and First Gold. Peter says of his beer taste:

I'm old-fashioned. I don't like things like fruit beers. I like beer just to have hops, malt, yeast and liquor. I believe that there is no such thing as bad beer, just beer that has been badly kept.

Rail Ale is a light session beer, a fruity little number, which Peter believes is closest to the northern beers of his youth, while Piston is a malt-accented best bitter with a dry finish. According to Peter he wanted to make a similar beer to Wadworth's 6X, but with more bitterness. The beer is also bottled for the brewery by Bridport's Palmers. These are the two regular beers which are on offer all the time. Others include the strong dark brown Heavy Sleeper and the Christmas special Whistlemas, plus occasional specials such as a porter. Top rail ales indeed.

Beers: Rail Ale (3.8%); Piston Bitter (4.3%); Heavy Sleeper (5.4%); Whistlemas (strength varies from 6.3% to 7.3%). Bottles: Piston Bitter.

Star Beer: Heavy Sleeper (5.4%) – Mid-brown in colour, with its malty nose backed up by a hint of earthy hoppiness. On the palate it is fruity and malty before giving way to a lasting bitter finish with fruit remaining for some time.

Recommended outlet: The Beer Engine, Newton St Cyres.

Beer Festival

Event which celebrates beer and its many styles, usually lasting from one to four days. The idea emerged in the early-1970s when the success of CAMRA (Campaign for Real Ale) encouraged drinkers to try real ales from around the country. They are organised either by CAMRA or SIBA, a single pub with an enterprising landlord or a group of beer-loving individuals, often hoping to raise money for charity. Some CAMRA branches run festivals on a theme, such as Exeter and East Devon CAMRA's festival of winter ales in January. Breweries some-times organise their own festivals, with the most notable being the Celtic Beer Festival which is hosted by St Austell's in the atmospheric surroundings of the brewery cellars. The number of beer varieties sold can range from a dozen to well over 100, and dedicated beer tasters have been known to plan their weekends away to coincide with festi-vals. If you want to explore the rich diversity of Westcountry real ales, SIBA South West's Maltings Beer Festival is possibly the very best opportunity you will get to taste the beers and meet their brewers. It is held over three days every April at one of the few traditional maltings left in the country, Tuckers Maltings in Newton Abbot. (See **CAMRA, SIBA, Tuckers Maltings**.)

Drinkers at the Exeter and East Devon CAMRA Winter Beer Festival, held every January

Beer-mats

These are drip-mats once made from cork, but nowadays card is used. Breweries and organisations such as CAMRA and SIBA use them for promotional purposes. Beer-mat collectors are called 'tegestologists' and there is a Beer Mat Society with awards for the best beer-mats.

Big Sheep Brewery   Bideford, Devon

The Big Sheep tourist attraction may be better known for 'baas' of the ovine variety but it is also home to its own brewery, set up by Simon Lacey, who already had Country Life on the go at the nearby Pig on the Hill. His original plans were to brew Country Life beers at the pub and Big Sheep ones at the Big Sheep. However, he moved all his kit into the Big Sheep in May 2002 and has since produced all of Country Life beers plus developed the Big Sheep ones, including Baatenders Best (4.3%), a gorgeously fruity golden beer which is zesty and invigorating in the mouth before a long dry and bitter-sweet finish. Other beers Simon hopes to brew include Golden Fleece (4.5%) and Ram Raiders (7%). Simon can be seen at work in the brewery and there is also a shop where bottled beers can be bought. (See **Country Life**.)

Simon Lacey at the Country Life/Black Sheep Brewery, where brewing can be viewed in between watching the sheep-shearing and duck-trials

Brewed and Bottled by Master Brewer Simon Lacey
The BIG Sheep Brewery,
Bideford, North Devon EX39 5AP
www.thebigsheep.co.uk

Originated at Lundy Island, and then expanded to 'The Pig on the Hill' pub, many awards later, the brewing moved to The BIG Sheep tourist attraction in 2002. The brewery is open to the public for tours and tasting. The tours, given by the brewer, offer a unique insight into the production of traditional real ales and is a popular stop especially with the dads. A retail outlet gives the visitors a chance to buy beers to take home.

Baatenders Best is a bottle conditioned beer, which means that the beer has not been pasteurised or carbonated. This is the best way to preserve the subtle flavours and aromas, giving it a similar taste to the draught beer. It is brewed using the finest Devon barley, malted at Tuckers Maltings, Newton Abbot. Fresh whole hops and the brewery's very own strain of yeast.

IMPORTANT
Baatenders needs to be allowed to settle and then poured in to a glass carefully without stopping. This allows the sediment to stay in the bottom of the bottle giving a crystal clear beer.
SERVE CHILLED
ENJOY!

2002 BAATENDERS BEST Amber Ale 500ml ℮ Alc 4.3% Vol

Birds of Prey

Raptors and hawks seem to have inspired most of the beer names for Cotleigh Brewery and they have a fine award-winning set of pubclips and beer-mats to show for it. The range includes Old Buzzard, Golden

Eagle, Goshawk, Hobby Ale, Peregrine Porter, Osprey, Merlin and Hawkshead – owls also feature heavily. Does this mean that as soon as the cooper has cooled, members of the brewery are out in the hills with their bird books and bins? Not really. Cotleigh might have an association with the Hawk and Owl Trust, but the bird names came about by accident, according to co-owner John Aries:

Tawny was the first brew, and after that it seemed sensible to stick to the bird theme and then mainly birds of prey, though sometimes we run out of them or find someone else has used them. But we certainly wouldn't stoop to using Vulture!

*Below left: Cotleigh Brewery's Old Buzzard
Below: Poster for Cotleigh Brewery's Hawkshead, celebrating eighteen years of brewing from 1979 to 1997*

Bitter

Originally this was a draught version of pale ale before developing into a style of beer on its own. It is a uniquely British beer, whose name is thought to have emerged in the early-twentieth century when brewers with large tied estates called their draught beers 'bitter' to differentiate them from the bottled pale ales. The great quality of a classic English bitter is the balance between the malt character, which produces a biscuity and nutty taste on the palate, as well as contributing to a dry finish, and the aroma, bitterness and fruitiness coming from the workings of the hop. (See **IPA, Pale Ale**.)

Bittering Hops

Certain hops which are used to give bitterness and dryness to the flavour of beer are added at the beginning of the boil. They are also called copper hops and kettle hops. (See **Aroma Hops, Hops.**)

Summerskills Brewery's Best Bitter, a uniquely British beer style

Blackawton Brewery   Saltash, Cornwall

Several years ago chemistry graduate Steve Brooks was working for the Fire Service in Exeter but he felt rather dissatisfied. To get away from things, he and his wife went travelling in Australia, later visiting San Francisco. Both places impressed Steve with their brew-pubs and beer, but before he could do anything about this, fate intervened – his wife became pregnant, and they decided to return to Blighty. Back home in the West Country, looking for something to do, Steve remembered the brew-pubs he had enjoyed and thought about setting up something himself. As it happened he discovered that Blackawton, the oldest brewery in Devon, was on the market.

Blackawton Brewery's 44 Special, named after Blackawton village's connection with the American troops who trained in the area for D-Day, and West Country Gold

Set up by Nigel Fitzhugh in 1977 near the village from which it takes its name, Blackawton was one of the pioneers of the micro-brewery revolution in the 1970s. The brewery was sold in the 1980s and moved to Washbourne near Totnes. By 2000 it was once more for sale, and Steve Brooks, having made a deal for the equipment and beer recipes, became the third owner. From Devon's oldest brewery it became one of Cornwall's youngest, when Steve moved the kit across the Tamar to his home near Saltash. Brewing at home did not work out because of planning problems, so the brewery moved once more to a nearby business park close to the A39. By the spring of 2002 Blackawton had moved again, to another site on the same business park, with the brewery now based in a concrete-built unit, with copper and mash tun at the front and fermenters in a back room.

The beers Steve makes are beautifully crafted and very drinkable. 'I'm a one-person band,' says Steve as he shows off his eight-barrel set-up. This includes converted dairy equipment from the 1930s-circa kit used in the early days of the brewery. It is supposed to have come from the old Tamar Brewery in Plymouth. Steve is also a deft handyman, making all the bits and bobs of brewing himself, such as a sparge arm which Barry Bucknell would have been proud of. When it comes to making beers, he continued with Blackawton's tried-and-trusted favourites: Blackawton Original Bitter, West Country Gold, 44 Special and Headstrong; these regulars have been joined by Exhibition Ale, which has been brewed for the Wetherspoon pub chain. They are fruity beers with an excellent balance of malt and hops which makes them very drinkable. Main hops used are Progress and Challenger which are top bittering hops, while Styrian Goldings and Cascade offer full aromatic and fruity noses. Fuggles (as well as coriander) is also added to the Easter special Wheal Dream. Other seasonal specials include Winter Fuel which uses mace, aniseed and liquorice to give a warming feel to the brew. Steve says:

Blackawton 44 Special as it appeared in the 1990s, when it was based in Devon

> *I like to use herbs in my beers. For instance, I've always wanted to make a ginseng beer, while I've also an idea to use a Chinese root called wolf-berry. Apparently it is an aphrodisiac.*

Well that is one way of getting people to love your beers!

Beers: Blackawton Original Bitter (3.8%); West Country Gold (4.1%); 44 Special (4.5%); Exhibition (4.7%); Headstrong (5.2%). Occasional: Wheal Dream (4.1%); Winter Fuel (5%). Bottles: West Country Gold; Winter Fuel; Headstrong, all bottle-conditioned.

Star Beer: Headstrong (5.2%) – Dark-bronze beer with a wonderfully fruity nose which suggests Seville orange peel and grapefruit; there is also a suggestion of ripe melon. On the palate there is an initial biscuity maltiness before a perfumey hoppiness and citrus fruitiness take over, leading to a lingering finish which also has a striking bitterness. Deceptively drinkable and moreish for its strength.

Recommended outlets: The Great Western Hotel, Exeter; The Bridge, Topsham.

Blackdown Brewery   Dunkerswell, Devon

Five-barrel Blackdown Brewery is one of Devon's latest craft brewers, having fired up its copper in the summer of 2002. It is owned by SW Fabrications, a company in the Blackdown Hills who have made brewing kit for the likes of the Ring O' Bells, Princetown and Otter. 'The idea of a brewery had been gelling for a long time

A brand new mash tun at Blackdown Brewery

and we had a showpiece brewery standing idle,' says Steve Wardman, who runs the show with dad Bob and brother Phil. One of Somerset's most experienced and venerable brewers Ted Bishop (founder of Cotleigh) was lured away from his Wellington brewery Juwards, and invited to brew. 'The idea of a brewery had been gelling for a long time and we had Ted, who was a regular customer, in mind when the kit was being built,' says Steve, who confesses to being a former lager drinker.

According to plan, Ted was soon to be found by visitors to the brewery at Dunkerswell airfield, hidden away in the beautiful Blackdown Hills, happily 'playing' with his gleaming stainless steel kit. With the hot liquor tank at the top, the mash tun, copper and four fermenting vessels in two rooms on the first floor and space for casks and raw materials on the bottom, this is a small brewer's dream. First beer off the racks was Blackdown Best, a copper-coloured session beer which is dangerously drinkable. Hops are Challenger and Williamette, which when combined give a good aroma and a decent bitterness. Other beers to be produced include Blackdown Bitter and Blackdown Premium. Sadly, Ted and the Blackdown Brewery parted company in August 2002, with Steve taking over brewing.

Beers: Blackdown Bitter (3.8%); Blackdown Best (4%); Blackdown Gold (4.3%); Blackdown Premium (4.7%).

Star Beer: Blackdown Gold (4.3%) – Lusciously fruity golden ale. The nose is tropical fruit (pineapple) plus hoppiness. On the palate, there is some malt kicking off the show, but it is very much the lipsmackingly fruitiness (pineapple, kiwi fruit) which steals the applause. There is a big bitter finish with a trace of fruit lingering along. Wonderful.

Recommended outlets: The Exeter Inn, Bampton; the Trout, Bickleigh.

Blewitt's Brewery   Kingsbridge, Devon

Years before he set up a brewery in his pub in Kingsbridge, Steve Blewitt was already getting the hang of the business. At the age of ten he was home-brewing and making his pocket money by selling it to his father. In 1988 he started doing it for real when he bought the Ship & Plough, a solid town pub nearly 200 years old:

Blewitt's Brewery with brewer Jeff Fredericks

I started off brewing behind the bar in a ten-gallon copper which was made from an old boiler. I would be doing the whole brew behind the bar while serving and the whole place stunk! After several months of this a larger copper was installed in a room above the pub. Then we moved out to Church Stow and set up in a unit, but that went wrong and we came back to the pub.

Blewitt's beers are currently produced at the Sorley Tunnel Adventure Farm, just outside Kingsbridge. This is an idyllic spot where the small kit is located in an old barn, part of which dates from the sixteenth century – the original arrow slits can still be seen. The other half of Blewitt's Brewery, brewer Jeff Fredericks, had originally brewed with Steve for several years in the 1990s. Having left in the mid-90s he kept in touch with Steve and returned in the autumn of 2001. Now, he and Steve are set to upgrade the plant to a five-barrel one and there are lots of other ideas as Jeff, who grew up in the former colony of Malaya, explains:

Sorley is an organic farm and next year will be fully organic. We have been given an acre to grow organic hops and there will also be organic barley here which we will send to be malted. I have a great love of the English countryside and traditions, and I love the idea of our beer coming from here, the place where we are sited.

Below left: *The idyllic home of Blewitt's Brewery*
Below: *Inside Blewitt's Brewery with brewer Jeff Fredericks checking a fermenting vessel*

Other plans also include a beer hall, where visitors to the brewery can sample the beers. Currently, Jeff produces four Blewitt's beers, though back in the 1990s there were all sorts of different ones, including a strawberry beer. Hops used are Challenger, Goldings and Fuggles, so there are plenty of fruity flavours. The session beer is Blewitt's Best. Blewitt's Wages is a pale best bitter which Jeff aims at young lager drinkers in the hope of weening them on to bitter. Then there's Blewitt's Head Off and Blewitt's Top, which is described as a very malty winter beer. There are other beers from time to time. Unlike many Westcountry brewers, Jeff goes easy on the hops which means that the beers are fruity and well-rounded but not as bitter as some in the region. Steve's surname is also very useful as all the beers can have a memorable play on his name. Though as Jeff says, 'We've had to modify the really cheeky names, people end up being reluctant to ask for them if they're a bit rude.'

During the 1997 election campaign, Blewitt's penchant for names got them into the *News of the World* when the beer Major Blewitt attracted

The Ship & Plough, Kingsbridge, where Blewitt's beers can be sampled

a lot of media attention. 'It also got the beer into the House of Commons, so that can't be bad,' recalls Jeff.

Beers: Blewitt's Best (3.5%); Blewitt's Wages (4.5%); Blewitt's Head Off (5%). Occasional: Blewitt's Top (5%).

Star Beer: Blewitt's Head Off (5%) – Chestnut-brown strong beer with malt and fruit on the nose. On the palate, there's a good malt character, with a fruitiness coming through mid palate. It is also very full-bodied. The finish is bitter with more fruit and hints of malt.

Recommended outlet: Ship & Plough, Kingsbridge.

Blue Anchor Brew-pub   Helston, Cornwall

The Blue Anchor occupies a distinctive niche in British brewing history. According to landlord Simon Stone, who has been in residence since 1993, the Blue Anchor has been continuously brewing for 160 years, with some of its current equipment going back to the years before the First World War. Its history, however, goes back much further. In the Middle Ages it was a rest-house run by monks, where weary travellers could get sustenance. Then it became a tavern and has remained that way for over 500 years. It has been an eventful time: there have been two suicides, and in 1717 the landlord was murdered. During the 1800s it was a popular place with local tin miners who had their wages paid out at the inn, with calamitous results for their families who found the week's housekeeping vanishing down their husbands' throats. In the 1970s, it was one of only four surviving brew-pubs in the whole country. Since then it has become a mecca for lovers of beer and traditional pubs. Tim Sears is the brewer and has been carefully nuturing the Blue Anchor's 'Spingo' beers for over twenty years now, as he recalls:

I was into home-brewing and heard that there was a vacancy going. They took me on a six-week trial and I suppose I have the job though no one has ever said anything.

Inside the Blue Anchor fermenting room with Alan Rowe, one half of an idiosyncratic brewing team

He is helped by Alan Rowe, another former home-brewer, who joined up in 2001. 'When you have an opportunity like this you say yes please,' he says. Together the two of them produce exceptionally strong and distinctive Cornish beers which all have the generic name of Spingo, an old Victorian name for strong ale (in Yorkshire, they used to call similar beers Stingo). The beers they brew are legendary, some of them regarded as the absinthe of Cornwall. Their two main beers are Middle and Special, and they also produce a special very strong Easter and Christmas beer, while Braggart or Spingo 800 is a hopless ale flavoured with honey and apple juice. This was produced in 2001 for the 800th anniversary of King John granting Helston its first charter. 'This has met with general approval,' says Tim, 'it is sweet, smooth and

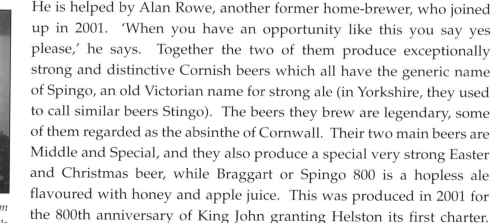

deceptively strong.' The strength of the Spingo beers apparently dates from the end of the First World War according to Tim:

Above left: The Blue Anchor: the brewery's wooden mash tun which has such a chequered history
Above: Blue Anchor Brewery with a new brew going through the cooling process before descending to the fermenting vessels in the room below

The story about Middle was that it was produced by the landlord to welcome home the troops who wanted a good strong ale. After that the Blue Anchor developed that reputation for beers that are a touch more alcoholic than most.

The tiny brew-house, at the back of the pub, is the domain of Tim and Alan, who sometimes come across as the Reeves and Mortimer of the brewing world. When Tim is asked how he got into the brewery, Alan answers, 'through the front door'. Other questions are met with equally odd and obtuse answers. Upstairs, there is the mash tun, an old copper, cooler tray, collecting vessel, with the fermenting vessels downstairs. The mash tun is made from oak, and apparently fell off the back of a boat some time in the early years of the twentieth century. 'It was full of French red wine,' says Tim who is writing a book about the Blue Anchor. 'The contents were sold and it ended up in here. Or so I'm told.' Tim brews two or three times during the winter and four in the summer. Goldings is the only hop used, while pale and crystal malt go into the grist. Yeast is skimmed off the top of each brew and used for the next one, while the water comes from a well beneath the corridor which runs through the pub. 'It is very much a traditional brewery,' says Tim, who admits that brewing at the Blue Anchor is certainly very different from his last job: retail. The Blue Anchor is one of the treasures of the West Country and if you only visit one pub and drink one brewery's beers then this is the place.

Beers: Jubilee (4.5%); Middle (5%); Braggert (6%); Special (6.6%). Occasional: Easter and Christmas Special (7.5%); Bottles: Middle; Braggert; Special, all bottle-conditioned.

Star Beer: Special (6.6%) – A dark-mahogany colour with an excitingly complex nose which hints at marshmallows, toffee ice-cream, caramel and the faintest suggestion of crème brûlée. The palate has a winey, port-like quality, but it also has baked banana, some nuttiness, toffee, estery notes and alcohol, before going into a bitter-sweet, dry and spicy finish. A beer to contemplate as the world passes by, but also dangerously drinkable.

Recommended outlet: The Blue Anchor, Helston.

Bodmin Ales

One-man brewing operation set up in December 1982 by John Holden on a former pig farm at Cardinham on Bodmin Moor. Prior to moving out to Cornwall, John Holden was landlord at the Bell in Bishop's Lydeard, near Taunton, Somerset, where he also had a small brewery. His first beer was Bell Bitter (OG 1038), named after his former pub. The brewery closed in 1984.

Bog Myrtle

Before hops, herbs such as Bog Myrtle were added to ale to balance the sweetness. In recent years enterprising brewers have reintroduced it as a bittering agent in specialist beers. Devon's O'Hanlon's use it to flavour their Myrica ale (4.2%), with stocks being harvested from freely growing plants over the water in Kerry.

St Austell's 1851, just one of many bottle-conditioned beers in the West Country

Bottle-conditioning

Bottle-conditioned beers are live beers bottled with a yeast sediment so they continue maturing, and their flavour deepens. Real ale in a bottle, in other words. Some brewers bottle straight from cask, though the quality can be very hit and miss. Others filter out old yeast and add fresh yeast, while some 'krasen' their beer which means the addition of partially fermented wort giving the yeast more fermentable sugars to snack on. The more care a brewer takes, then the better the beer will be. These are beers which continue to mature in the bottle, developing more rounded and deeper flavours.

Bottom Fermentation

Style of fermentation where the yeast sinks to the bottom of the fermenting vessel and works at a lower temperature than top fermentation – rightly it should be called lager fermentation. Mainly used for lager production, though Otter Brewery use it for producing their ales. (See **Lager, Top Fermentation, Yeast**.)

Boys' Bitter

Low-alcohol, lightly hopped but refreshing Westcountry bitter which was supposed to ween teenagers on to the taste of beer in the days before lager and alco-pops. Examples included Courage's BA, St

Austell's BB and Palmer's Bridport Bitter. They were light in taste, gravity and alcohol and very refreshing. If you had done a hard day's work, then the last thing you wanted to do was get stuck into a 6% beer.

Branscombe Vale Brewery   Branscombe, Devon

Brewers Graham Luxton and Paul Dimond make their wonderful beers in old farm buildings leased from the National Trust. The South-West Coast Path passes by their front door so if they ever get bored they can look out over the sea and watch its ever changing moods. The beautiful village of Branscombe is also very near, which is just as well as the Fountain Head, found at the other end of this elongated village, is the unofficial brewery tap for Branscombe. Before they set up the brewery in 1992, Graham and Paul worked for dairy firms, but Graham had been thinking about a change for a while. 'It had been in my mind since the 1980s when I used to go to the Beer Engine,' he says. 'I had married into the pub (Graham's wife's family had run the Fountain Head for years) and I originally thought about a brew-pub. I thought it would be a good idea, but I had a family and a job.' Then he met Paul who was working at Express Foods as well and the two of them thought they would have a go. First, though, they had to do a lot of research, which meant going round pubs in the area, tasting the beers and eating the peanuts. As luck would have it, their plans received a boost when they were made redundant in early-1992, and they ended up leasing part of an old farm from the National Trust. They dug their own well to obtain spring water, got hold of the necessary kit and started brewing in September 1992.

Beginning as a five-barrel outfit, they have now doubled their capacity and sell beers all over Dorset, Devon and Somerset. During the winter months they brew three times a week, and in the summer four-and-a-half times a week. Beers in this part of the world traditionally used to possess a certain sweetness in the finish, but Branscombe's beers are dry and hoppy with plenty of fruity flavours. Their first beer was Branoc Bitter, after the original name of Branscombe village and its attendant Celtic Saint. This was accompanied by Olde Stoker, a lovely rich dark winter beer. Sadly, it is not available anymore. These days Branoc is joined at the pumps by the well-rounded best bitter Drayman's, which Paul says is the 'smoothest beer we do', and an own-label beer, which goes out to pubs under whatever name the customer chooses. Seasonal beers include the dark, strong mild Hells Belles, the dangerously drinkable Yo Ho Ho and a popular summer beer Summa That. They have also produced a lager with the name Horn, while their mild is called BUM – you don't need much of an imagination to picture that pumpclip.

Above: *Branscombe Vale Brewery, where the South-West Coast Path passes by the front door*
Above right: *Inside the Branscombe Vale Brewery, with Graham Luxton* (left) *and Paul Dimond*

'Images started off as professional,' laughs Paul, 'but at the end you've got to laugh at yourself.' Apart from the Fountain Head and the Old Inn at Kilmington, which was opened by the brewery in spring 2002, one of the best places to get Branscombe's beer is the much cherished Bridge Inn at Topsham, near Exeter. The Queen visited several years back and Branscombe was commissioned to brew a special beer for the occasion and invited to attend the event. 'It was a weird day,' recalls Graham, 'there were lots of security crawling around the place but we were OK. We sat in the garden drinking.' Her Majesty was also given a case to take home with her. One can only hope it was not one of BUM.

Beers: Branoc Bitter (3.8%); Drayman's Best Bitter (4.2%); Own Label (4.6%). Occasional: BUM (3.3%); Anniversary Ale (4.6%); Horn Lager (4.7%); Hells Belles (4.8%); Summa That (5%); Yo Ho Ho (6%). Bottles: Drayman's Best Bitter, bottle-conditioned.

Star Beer: Summa That (5%) – Straw-coloured summer beer with a good lemony, fruity nose and a subtle dash of biscuit malt in the background. Plenty of fruit and hops make for a lively and refreshing encounter on the palate, before a long, bitter finish with plenty of hop character.

Recommended pubs: The Bridge Inn, Topsham; the Fountain Head, Branscombe.

Brewing

Even though some brewers do their best to make their job a mystery, brewing beer is a fairly simple process, somewhat akin to making a pot of tea. First of all, crushed malt (the grist) is steeped in hot water in the mash tun for anything up to a couple of hours. This is called mashing. For light beers, this will be pale malt (the main malt used) with a dash of crystal malt for body and slight colour. Other malts, including roast barley, black malt and chocolate malt, are also added in handfuls for colour and extra flavour. During this time the liquor (as water is called in brewing terms) extracts the fermentable sugars from the malt. After

the mash is finished, the malt is sparged (or sprayed) with hot water to extract any remaining sugars. The malt is then removed from the mash tun and usually fed to cows and pigs. The liquid which remains is called the wort and tastes a bit like Ovaltine. It is transferred to the copper where it will be boiled with hops for up to ninety minutes. Hops are added at the beginning, middle and often at the end. Think of them as condiments – the skill of the brewer is to add the right hops at the right time. Other ingredients added during the boil could include fruit, spices, licquorice and even chocolate.

Clockwise, starting top left: Grist being sparged at St Austell; Late aroma hops are put into the copper by Black Sheep/Country Life brewer Simon Lacey; Fermenting squares at Norman & Pring; Filling barrels or racking at St Austell

After the boil, the hopped wort (as it is now known) is transferred through a cooling system before being pumped into a fermenting vessel. Here yeast is pitched into the cooled beer and the process of fermentation begins. The yeast attacks the fermentable sugars in the hopped wort, turning them into alcohol. Carbon dioxide is also generated. The more malt that is used and the accompanying higher level of fermentable sugars, then the higher level of alcohol you get. The beer stays in the fermenting vessel for between four to seven days, depending on the brewery, and it is then transferred into brewery conditioning tanks or casks (this process is called racking). Further maturation continues with the rough edges of the green beer being smoothed out.

When in cask it undergoes a secondary fermentation and finings are added to clear the beer. Some brewers like to add hop pellets to their casks before they are sealed. This is called dry-hopping and gives an extra hoppiness to their beers. See, it is not that mysterious after all. (See **Aroma Hops, Bittering Hops, Burtonisation, Flavour, Hops, Malt, Yeast, Water**.)

Breweriana

Some people collect beer-mats, others pumpclips or bar towels and those with lots of space spend their spare time tracking down bottles. We are talking about breweriana, which is the word given to those collectible items to do with pubs, beer, brewing and drinking. Anything is fair game, from the above mentioned to ashtrays, adverts, bottle tops, beer labels and books. Especially desirable are those bits of breweriana linked with breweries now gone for good. (See **Beer-mats, Pumpclips**.)

Brown Ale

Nutty, dry and fruity, beer particular to the North East of England, as represented by the world-famous Newcastle Brown and Double Maxim. Once, a lot of breweries made brown ales as part of their portfolio, with southern ones being darker and sweeter than their northern cousins. Nut Brown Ale was another name, presumably because of the nutty flavours present. The likes of Heavitree, Norman & Pring and St Austell all used to make brown ales.

Burton Ales

Until the 1950s, this was the name given to a strong, dark beer which was available during the winter. Burtons varied in flavour, some being quite strongly hopped, while others were strong milds.

Burtonisation

In the Middle Ages, monks started brewing beer in Burton upon Trent and they discovered that the local well water was particularly excellent for their purposes. By the nineteenth century, Burton had become the brewing centre of England, and its beers were revered everywhere – the local water possessing a range of mineral salts, especially gypsum, which was perfect for the pale ales and bitters which swept the English pubs and bars of the late-nineteenth century. Brewers from across the country noticed this trend and added similar mineral salts to their brewing liquor, which enabled them to produce beers similar to those of Burton's breweries. This was called Burtonising and continues to this day.

No longer produced, St Austell Brown Ale

C *is for*
CAMRA, country brews (and cheers!)...

CAMRA

Without the Campaign for Real Ale, there would be no real ale, and fizzy and flavourless beer would be our common lot. Opening time began in 1971, when four English drinkers on holiday in Ireland were bemoaning the state of ale back home. They decided to do something about it and formed the Campaign for the Revitalisation of Ale – it was a bit of a laugh at first but hit a chord among drinkers, fed up with favourite pubs being gutted and turned into chintzy living rooms, while locally brewed beers were replaced by a gassy product made in a factory hundreds of miles away. In 1973, 1000 members had signed the pledge to save British beer, but the title was seen as too much of a mouthful. So the Campaign for Real Ale was born. Since then it has fought pub and brewery closures, celebrated the small-brewers' boom, held hundreds of beer festivals across the country, lobbied governments about such issues as the Beer Orders, Short Measures and Guest Ales and generally saved British cask-conditioned ale from becoming a small minority taste such as pear perry or mead. These days, membership tops 60 000 and the organisation has been doing its utmost to shed its beer-bellies and woolly-jumpers image – at least 25 per cent of the membership is female. As a campaigning group it is unparalleled in the brewing world, and it went on to influence small brewers across the world, especially in America. Its showpiece, the Great British Beer Festival, is held every August at Olympia and it publishes a newspaper, *What's Brewing*, where you can keep abreast of what is going on in the brewing world. In Devon and Cornwall, there are five branches, whose members organise beer festivals, arrange social events in local pubs, campaign for real ale and generally keep the flag flying. (See **Real Ale**.)

W & EC Carne   Falmouth, Devon

Busy brewery set up in the second half of the nineteenth century, where wine, corn and rope were jostling for space with barrels of beer and porter. If that was not enough, they were also ship-brokers. In 1921, Carne was swallowed up by JA Devenish. Brewing ceased in 1926,

Festival fun: the South Devon CAMRA Beer Festival happens every autumn

An oversized Devenish beer-mat recalling former Falmouth brewery Carne's

when the premises were replaced by an Odeon cinema. Devenish produced a keg beer called Carne's Falmouth Bitter back in the 1980s.

Carr & Quick   Exeter, Devon

This company took over brewing operations at the West of England Brewery in Okehampton Street, having bought it up in 1909. The plant had originally begun production as Mortimore's in 1878 before passing to William Henry Morton in 1906. There were also seven pubs, while the beers produced included an Oatmeal Stout. Carr & Quick stopped brewing in 1927, but continued in business as beer, wine and spirit merchants. (See **William Henry Morton**.)

Charity

Many breweries are part and parcel of Westcountry life, involving themselves in local events and charities. For instance, Exmoor Ales sponsors the Exmoor National Parks Partnership, which helps maintain Park paths. Exe Valley Brewery brewed Curate's Choice (4.8%), which, as Guy Sheppard at the brewery explained:

…was made to celebrate my wife's ordination as a deacon. For every pint sold, 5p was donated to the local hospice in Exeter. It generated £1900. The Church were very happy with it, after all it was an old tradition with church ales.

Quaff for charity with St Austell's Sunrise

In Cornwall, St Austell brewed Sunrise (3.9%), a summer ale in support of the Treliske Hospital Sunrise appeal for a cancer unit. For every pint of beer sold, 5p was donated to the appeal. Football teams are supported, while special beers and beer festivals raise money for favoured charities. Brewers are businessmen and women first and foremost, but they are also part of the local community and try to put something back in.

Pubs have also long been fund-raisers. In the 1950s and 60s, piles of pennies were popular ways of raising money, with local celebrities sometimes being brought in to knock down the heap. On one memorable occasion, the then captain of Exeter City FC was pictured wearing football boots with his suit as he kicked down a pile in a Norman & Pring pub.

Church Ales

Community celebration in the Middle Ages where churchwardens organised the brewing of a quantity of beer with malt donated by the local farmers. This was then sold to the locals to raise funds for the Church. Some parishes had a church-house where spits, cooking utensils and brewing equipment were stored; some of these eventually developed into church-house inns. Several can be found under that name in Devon today, such as the Church House Inn at Holne on the edge of Dartmoor. There were also other bouts of ale-inspired merry-making such as bede ales, help ales, cuckoo ales, bride ales and Whitsun ales.

Clearwater Brewery   Great Torrington, Devon

Over three centuries ago, this small town, sited on the top of a cliff rising from the meadows of the Torridge River, was a battle zone. The English Civil War was raging and after a major battle in 1646, many of the defeated Royalists were imprisoned in the local church. When it blew up major casualties inevitably ensued. Nowadays, things are rather more peaceful, but the period is remembered by a series of beers produced by Brian Broughton at Clearwater Brewery, which can be found in an industrial estate on the edge of town. Essex-born Brian came down to the West Country to work as a plumber in the 1980s but he was also a keen home-brewer and started the Ilfracombe-based Combe Brewery in 1993. After a couple of years, that folded and he returned to plumbing. The plant was then sold to Tim Webster who set up Barum in Barnstaple. Brian was soon in the thick of the fray, again helping out at Barum before taking a second crack at brewing with Clearwater in 1999, using equipment from the closed St Giles in The Wood Brewery. Brian recalls:

My ambition was to make it successful, and I did 16 different beers on the trot, all called after fish. These were narrowed down to five, including Minnow [3.6%] and Sea Trout [4%]. Then I decided to revamp the beers' images to suit a local theme and as Torrington was trying to make 1646 a selling point I thought I'd go along with it.

Oliver Cromwell led the Roundhead's cavalry in their defeat of the Royalists at Marston Moor in 1643. One of the last battles of the Civil War took place in Torrington in 1646. He went on to be **Protector** of England, supported by his New Model Army.

BEST SERVED SLIGHTLY CHILLED

Best before

CLEARWATER BREWERY • TORRINGTON

Abv 5.2%

OLIVER'S NECTAR

Clearwater Brewery is a very young brewery. We consider ourselves as traditionalists in the way we brew, using only natural ingredients, Whole Hops, Malted Barley and Yeast. Great care is taken on each brew to produce this fine nectar.

There will be a harmless deposit of yeast and care should be taken when pouring beer into a glass. Gentle pouring will produce a clear beer for you to savour.

Cheers!

Brewing matters did not always proceed quite as they should. For instance, Torrington Old English Ale happened quite by accident, after Brian started a day's brewing following a night spent, as he says, 'checking quality control'. He was supposed to be brewing 1646, but without checking he started pouring what he thought was pale malt into the hot liquor when the grist suddenly went black. He had put in the wrong malt. Instead of pale, half a bag of dark chocolate malt had been poured into the mash. It was too late to do anything else about it and he turned to the pale malt for the rest of the grist. He had managed to produce a successful winter porter, but there was one problem – it was summer.

Clearwater is a two-man operation, with Ray Thomas helping out on general brewery duties and deliveries, while Brian does the brewing. It is a ten-barrel plant, with Challenger, East Kent Goldings, Fuggles, Brambling Cross, Mount Hood and Target being the hops used. Brian says:

Brian Broughton, Clearwater Brewery, doing a bit of quality control

I love bitter beers with nice hoppy aromas, but I don't produce beers for my palate. Cavalier, which has a good hoppy bitterness in the finish, and Oliver's Nectar, which has a subtle bitterness in the finish, are both to my liking. The beers in the middle are made to how the public like it, slightly sweeter and more malty.

(See **Combe Brewery**.)

Beers: Cavalier (4%); Rambler's Special (4.4%); 1646 (4.8%); Oliver's Nectar (5.2%). Occasional: Beggar's Tipple (4.2%); Torrington Old English Ale (4.8%); Yule Remember (4.8%). Bottles: Cavalier, 1646; Oliver's Nectar, all bottle-conditioned.

Star Beer: 1646 (4.8%) – Dark-gold, orange-marmalade colour. The nose of this premium bitter has a citrusy fruitiness, including hints of lemon, with an underlying soft biscuity maltiness. The palate has plenty of flavour with citrusy fruitiness well to the fore (orange peel?), followed by a pleasing tangy hoppiness, finally leading to a lingering bitter and fruity finish with some suggestions of sweetness. A complex beer to be studied at length.

Recommended pubs: The Crown Hotel, Lynton; The Clinton Arms, Frithelstock, near Great Torrington.

One of Combe Brewery's seasonal beers

Combe Brewery   Ilfracombe, Devon

Short-lived five-barrel brewery started by Brian Broughton in Ilfracombe in the autumn of 1994. Two years later it closed. Beers produced included Heatwave (3.7%), Combe Gold (4%), Shipwrecker's Ale (4.4%) and Wallop (5%). (See **Clearwater**.)

Cooper

Beer was traditionally kept in wooden casks, and the cooper was the man who repaired and made these casks. It is a dying trade these days, with very few employed by breweries. Llew Jones, who was the last cooper at St Austell, retired in 2001.

A message from St Austell's final cooper on his last barrel in 2001

Copper

Brewing vessel, usually stainless steel, in which the wort is boiled and hops and other flavourings are added. Also called the kettle. (See **Brewing, Mash.**)

Cornish Brewery   Redruth, Cornwall

See JA Devenish.

G Crake   Plymouth, Devon

Began brewing in 1820, but nearly 100 years later Reading brewers Simonds bought the business, along with a pub estate of nearly 30 houses. (See **Tamar Brewery**.)

Above left: Simon Lacey checks the copper at the Country Life/Black Sheep Brewery
Above: Ring O' Bells Adrian Carter with the brewery's splendidly shiny copper

Creedy Valley Brewery   Crediton, Devon

This short-lived venture was set up in 1984 by Henry Drew and Brian Bell. Both worked for Whitbread in Tiverton before it closed. The brewery's home was a converted gasworks and the two men built their own 12-barrel plant, producing three beers: Creedy Bitter (OG 1036), Tun Bitter (OG 1041) and Taverners Ale (OG 1045). Times were tough from the start, according to Henry Drew in September 1984. 'We are rather late in the field and many local pubs already take beers from other small breweries,' he said. Unfortunately, this was a sign of the future as the brewery closed down in 1985.

Crocombe & Son   Parracombe, Devon

Originally maltsters, the Crocombe family started brewing in the 1870s and this became the main business. There was also a tied estate of 16 pubs. Brewing continued until 1940 when the head of the company died and the business was wrapped up. Interestingly enough, this part of North Devon had a chapel-led reputation for looking down on all matters alcoholic, with many pubs in the nineteenth century being bought up and closed. This, apparently, is why very few 'olde worlde' rural pubs are to be found in this part of the world.

Cotleigh Brewery – John and Jenny Aries

Cotleigh Brewery   Wiveliscombe, Somerset

Husband-and-wife team John and Jenny Aries have run Cotleigh since the early-1980s. However, the brewery started life in 1979 when it was set up by former Navy man Ted Bishop. Ted, who until recently brewed for the Blackdown Brewery, built a five-barrel plant at a Devon farmhouse not far from Tiverton, but demand for the beer quickly far exceeded capacity. A year later Cotleigh moved to Wiveliscombe and found themselves sharing part of the old Arnold & Hancock's building with another brewery, Golden Hill, later Exmoor Ales. At that time, John Aries was spending his time on leave from the Merchant Navy helping out part-time. In 1982 Ted left and John took over. 'I was in charge of the business and conned my girlfriend to become my business partner and later on my wife,' he says. The two of them had met when Jenny was pulling pints at a pub. She asked him if he liked the beer he'd drunk and would he like another. He said yes, and then told her that he also brewed it!

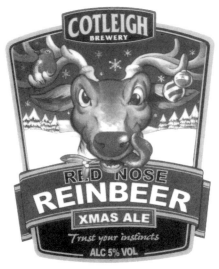

A sleigher of a beer: Cotleigh Brewery's Red Nose Reinbeer

In 1985 Cotleigh moved to their present home just down the hill from their old premises. Nowadays, Cotleigh are one of the more successful and larger craft breweries. Their beers are found all over the West Country and, thanks to the Wetherspoon pub chain, throughout the UK. They have a staff of nine, including head brewer Andy Greenbank, who used to work at Exmoor Ales. Malt comes from the

West Country. Hops are mainly English, apart from several intriguing beers brewed with hops from the USA, Australia and New Zealand. Along with yeast and water, nothing else goes into their well-rounded, hoppy ales. Session bitter Tawny was the first beer to be produced by Cotleigh, and it is a wonderful beverage with plenty of malt and hop character. Then there is the golden beer Golden Eagle, best bitter Barn Owl and the excellent dark ale Old Buzzard, available through the winter months. There are also monthly guest beers. 'The guest beer is our chance to experiment,' says John. 'It might be just using one malt, often it is using just one of the varieties of the hops.'

John and Jenny, who live locally, have always been very keen in putting something back into the community. The local football team is supported, while their adopted charity is the Hawk & Owl Trust, for whom they have raised a significant amount of money. The brewery have also unveiled their first dray which is occasionally used for local deliveries. Once a regular sight in Wiveliscombe during the days of Hancock's, it is a sign of how seriously Cotleigh take their place in the town's brewing history. John says:

We are still brewing the way they brewed at the top of the hill 150 years ago. We have better control, but it is still very much a look-and-sniff operation. The junior brewer comes in on Saturday morning, walks around the fermenting vessels, has a look at the beer, then spends the next couple of hours, taking samples, reading the gravity, taking temperatures and confirming what he knew using his eyes and nose.

Beers: Tawny (3.8%); Golden Eagle (4.2%); Barn Owl (4.5%); Old Buzzard (4.8%), winter only. Occasional: Kiwi Pale Ale (3.9%); Harvest Ale (4%); Blue Jay Best Bitter (4.2%); Kookaburra Premium Ale (4.4%); Peregrine Porter (4.4%); Snowy Winter Ale (5%); Osprey Strong Ale (5%); Red Nose Reinbeer (5%). Bottles: Old Buzzard, bottle-conditioned.
Star Beer: Barn Owl (4.5%) – Well-flavoured best bitter with fruit (reminiscent of peach) and undertones of malt on the nose. At the beginning of the palate there is a nuttiness and maltiness which is balanced by the development of a fresh fruitiness and hoppiness. The finish has a lasting bitterness with more fruitiness in it. Launched in 1994 and immediately won Supreme Champion at the Tuckers Maltings festival.
Recommended pubs: The Butterleigh Inn, Butterleigh; Prince of Wales, Holcombe Rogus.

Country Life Brewery   The Big Sheep, Bideford, Devon

Working with your in-laws is not always a recipe for success, but that

Country Life's Simon filling barrels at the Pig on the Hill before the move to the Big Sheep

was not the case for Simon Lacey who started the Country Life Brewery at the Pig on the Hill pub, which is owned by his wife's parents. It all began when he came out of the Royal Engineers in 1997 and went to work at the pub. As it happened, his in-laws had bought up the brewing kit from the defunct Lundy Island brewery. It was stored away in a garage and something had to be done. An extension was built at the back of the pub and, using a video which had been shot of the brewery in situ on Lundy, Simon set it up and started brewing. 'I began brewing in April 1998 and it became drinkable a couple of months later,' says Simon, who is also dead keen on marathon running and surfing. At first the plant was 2.5 barrels but demand soon saw it increase to five barrels.

Starting off brewing at the pub definitely had its advantages as his beers could hog the handpumps. 'In the early days,' recalls Simon, 'the pub was ideal to test the beers out on people and it was great to see their reactions.' First out of the fermenting vessels was a dark-golden beer called Golden Pig which started off at 5.7% but is now a more manageable 4.7%. The pig name and some of the motifs that occur on the beers' pumpclips are a tribute to the pigs kept at the pub. 'There have always been pigs there,' says Simon. 'The one at the moment is called Rodney Trotter.'

Other beers include the hoppy session beer Old Appledore, which came about when pubs in the nearby coastal village asked for a real ale for their local beer festival, and Wallop. This is a pale summer beer with a very aromatic grapefruit nose and plenty of fruitiness on the palate. It won an award at the Tuckers Maltings Beer Festival in 2000. 'My beers are very bitter beers,' says Simon who hops with Goldings, Fuggles and Challenger, 'but there's also a good fruitiness to them.' Special ales include the Yuletide visitor Old Nick, and the blockbusting Red Eye, brewed for the Potwalloping Festival at Westward Ho! This event is something that the Victorians dreamt up. Westward Ho! has a sandy beach and pebble ridge, and in the summer the festival sees locals and visitors throw all the stray pebbles back on to the ridge.

In the summer of 2002, Simon moved the brewery to the Big Sheep, a theme park devoted to all things ovine. Space at the Pig on the Hill was at a premium. Here he brews beers for both Country Life and a new operation called the Big Sheep Brewery, totally different beers from Country Life. The brewery is part of the Big Sheep's attractions, so in between watching the sheep-shearing and dogs rounding up ducks, keep an eye out for Simon at work behind a glass partition – unless he is out running, of course. (See **Big Sheep Brewery**.)

Beers: Old Appledore (3.7%); Golden Pig (4.7%); Country Bumpkin (5.7%). Occasional: Wallop (4.4%); Old Nick (5.2%), Red Eye (8.5%). Bottles: Old Appledore; Wallop; Golden Pig; Country Bumpkin; bottle-conditioned or filtered and carbonated.

Star Beer: Golden Pig (4.7%) – A wonderful citric fruit hop nose, which even has hints of marmalade, introduces this beer. The palate has grainy maltiness and an almost lemony fruitiness before descending into a dry and lasting bitterness thanks to the use of Challenger as the bittering hop.

Recommended pubs: Pig on the Hill, Pusehill, Westward Ho!; The Appledore Inn, Bideford.

D *is for*
drinks in the Doghouse...

Here comes the bride's beer: Devenish's Wedding Ale

Dawlish Brewery   Dawlish, Devon

Brewing started in 1817 at Dawlish High Street and by the end of the century the brewery owned over 20 pubs. Brewing came to an end in 1926 when Heavitree of Exeter bought the business.

JA Devenish   Redruth, Cornwall

Devenish started brewing in Weymouth in 1742, but in the twentieth century it snapped up several Cornish and Devon breweries, along with their pubs, thus being able to sell its beers right across the South West. Rumour has it that the brewery's owner used to sail his yacht from Weymouth to Cornwall and during one of these sojourns decided to try his luck at selling beer in the region. Breweries swallowed up by Devenish included Carne in Falmouth, Treluswell of Penryn and Vallance's of Sidmouth; the company bought up the Redruth Brewery in 1934 and began brewing on the site. In the 1980s, there were well over 300 Devenish pubs throughout the region, instantly identifiable by a heraldic tiger called Herbert who sported the company's unique green, gold and white livery. In the late-1960s and most of the 70s there were two main Devenish beers. According to one drinker of the time:

The ordinary bitter, named Devenish Bitter, was a fine quaffing ale at around only about 3.3%. The stronger ale at about 4.2% was called Cornish, and that was nice too. It was made in Redruth to the same recipe as Wessex, which was brewed in Weymouth, and sold in the pub estate over there. They also did a mild called XXX.

By 1985, Devenish quit brewing in Weymouth and moved all its brewing and bottling kit to Redruth, where it split into two arms. The brewing side was called the Cornish Brewery Company, while JA Devenish dealt with the pub estate. This state of affairs did not last long, as Devenish merged with the Inn Leisure Group. During this period the brewery became well known for its Newquay Steam Beers, a range of bottled pasteurised beers which were advertised as 'pure and natural'. They were available in Grolsch style bottles with stoppers. Along with the launch of the Newquay Steam, Devenish also produced a range of real ales, including JD Dry Hop Bitter (OG 1032), Cornish Original (OG 1038), Royal Wessex (OG 1042) and Great British Heavy (OG 1050).

The name Devenish finally vanished in the late-1980s when Greenall's acquired the pub estate, while the brewery was bought by the management and became known as Redruth again. (See **Redruth Brewery**.)

Dinner Ale

These were beers especially brewed to be drunk at home with a meal and enjoyed popularity in the early-twentieth century. They were low in alcohol and bottled. The yeast was usually filtered out and the beer was pasteurised; the absence of yeast sediment was seen as a selling point, and breweries' advertising always made reference to this fact. Luncheon and Family ales were of a similar ilk.

Plymouth Breweries price-list which includes Dinner Ale and Luncheon Stout

Doghouse Brewery   Scorrier, Cornwall

The Doghouse has to be one of the noisiest breweries one could ever visit, but we are not talking clanking machinery, the hiss of steam during the boil or the crashing of casks down a chute. Instead, the din really is produced by dogs. On arrival, over 100 barking dogs set up a background chorus as Ian Spencer-Brown displays the five-barrel kit he and Steve Willmott set up in the summer of 2001. It came from a closed brew-pub in the now defunct Firkin chain, called, aptly enough given the proximity of our canine pals, the Flea & Firkin. As well as being part of one of Cornwall's newest breweries, ex-RAF man Ian, originally from Kent, and his wife run a very successful boarding kennels, Startrax Pets Hotel. Ian explains:

We originally had boarding kennels with rescue dog kennels attached, then I decided I was just going to do ordinary boarding kennels. And that left me with 1000 square feet spare, so we knocked down the spare kennels and started up the brewery.

Long-term home-brewer and CAMRA activist Steve Willmott had known Ian for a number of years and the two of them got together. 'We went to a firm in Doncaster and bought the equipment,' remembers Ian, 'and brought it down and manhandled it in.' At the moment brewing takes place once a week, though Ian says they could easily do it four or five times a week. 'It is a two-man operation,' he says, 'and we find that sales and calling people and delivering takes up a lot of time.'

The Doghouse Brewery's Wet Nose, Bow Wow and Biter, yes that's the way to spell it

Not surprisingly, the brewery looks to the dog world for both its imagery and beer names. There are four regular beers, taking in golden hoppy session beers, malty best bitters and dark, strong knee-tremblers. The brewery's main beer and best seller is Loyal Corgi. This used to be called Royal Corgi until an email arrived from the Lord Chancellor's office objecting to the use of the prefix Royal. 'We started brewing it in March 2002 for the Jubilee, but it has become phenomenally successful so we'll have to think of a new name for it in 2003,' says Steve. The strongest regular beer Doghouse make is Bow Wow, which Steve says he modelled on Old Peculier, but it is not as strong as that infamous Yorkshire strong ale, nicknamed Lunatic's Broth. Among their occasional ales, a lager has also been made, which once brewed is lagered for a time, as all good lagers should. Doghouse also offers a service where a beer is named after a land-lord's dog, complete with specially designed pumpclips featuring a favourite mutt. 'Many pubs have a dog,' says Ian, who owns 12 Pyrenean mountain dogs, 'and we have beers with names like Old Arfur and Hell's Teeth.'

Even though the Doghouse is pretty new on the brewing scene, there are plans to bottle their beers and there may even be a pub in the pipeline in the near future. Just the place for a quiet pint, unlike the brewery!

Beers: Wet Nose (3.8%); Biter (4%); Loyal Corgi (4.5%); Bow Wow (5%). Occasional: Retriever (5%); Winter's Tail (5.8%); Christmas Tail (6.5%).

Star Beer: Loyal Corgi (4.5%) – Dark-gold in colour with an aro-matically fruity and hoppy nose and a dash of malt in the back-ground. On the palate a good malty character kicks off the tasting before a citrusy fruitiness (lemon, orange) joins in the fun, followed

Ian Spencer-Brown at work in the brewery

by a lingering dry and bitter finish. Plenty of flavour and eminently drinkable. Winner of Supreme Champion at the St Ives Beer Festival in 2002.

Recommended pubs: The Old Courthouse, Mawgan; The Hawkins Arms, Zelah.

Double Stout

Double or Extra stouts were strong, dark beers which were also known as Invalid Stouts. They were twice the strength of ordinary stouts. In the years before the First World War, stouts were seen as healthy, and many doctors prescribed these stouts for their convalescing patients as a restorative. (See **Porter, Stout**.)

Dray

Vehicle on which beer is transported. In the days before the motor engine, horse-drawn and steam-driven drays would have been a common sight in the towns and cities. Over in Wiveliscombe, Cotleigh Brewery recently unveiled their own horse-drawn dray which is occasionally used for local deliveries, shows and carnivals.

A steam-driven delivery for the Anchor Inn, Chudleigh, from Norman & Pring in 1900

A Norman & Pring drayhorse in the days before the motor engine

Norman & Pring delivery vans at the Crawford Hotel in Exeter

Driftwood Spars Hotel   Trevaunance Cove, St Agnes, Cornwall

Ask for a pint of Gordon's in the bar of this traditional and lively hotel and you will be given a beer rather than a mega measure of juniper-flavoured firewater. Gordon Treleaven has been brewing Cuckoo Ale since 2001, when he set up a small brewery with the kit from the closed Royal Inn & Horsebridge Brewery in Devon. 'We always wanted to do it,' says wife Jill, 'and when we bought the building across the way for conversion into bedrooms, there was room for a brewery.'

The Driftwood Spars has always been a noted place for its ales. The local CAMRA branch gave it a gold award for long-standing service to the cause of real ale and it has been runner-up in the branch's pub of the year competition. It is an historical building, originally built in the seventeenth century and during its life it has been a chandlers, ware-

Driftwood Spars Hotel, where Cuckoo Ale can be found

house and billet for war evacuees. It also has a bit of a reputation for its music. Queen played here before they became superstars, while Rod Stewart was supposed to have written Maggie May about a local girl. Other events at the hotel are more down to earth, as Jill explains:

We have a comic dog show where dogs win prizes for things such as the most peculiar looking dog or the one who eats the most daft things. We have had one dog which eats pickled onions.

The Cuckoo Ale is also an attraction. Brewed with Fuggles as the main hop, it is a mid-strength gently bitter beer, which is how Gordon likes his beers to taste. Up until the summer of 2002, this has been the only beer brewed as the kit has been too small. This was a bit of a problem as the Cuckoo Ale kept running out, which was frustrating for people who turned up especially for it. Thankfully, this should not last much longer as a brand-new, stainless steel, five-barrel kit has been built and is now up and running. Cuckoo Ale will still be brewed and be more available, while Jill reckons they might even be able to do two or three other beers. As for Cuckoo Ale, Jill explains the reason behind the name:

There's a legend about St Agnes that the locals tried to build a wall around a cuckoo so as to preserve eternal springtime, but it just flew away. Since then people out here have been known as cuckoo people and St Agnes as Cuckoo Land.

Beers: Cuckoo Ale (4.5–4.7%).
Star Beer: Cuckoo Ale (4.5–4.7%) – Mid-brown in colour with a malty and resiny hop nose. On the palate the malt character kicks in first, with hints of nuttiness, followed by a subtle fruitiness before the lasting but gently bitter finish.

Dry-Hopping

This is the practice of adding a handful of hops (or a hop pellet) to beer after it has been casked, which gives a fresh hop aroma and slightly increases the bitterness of the beer as it matures in the pub cellar. Westcountry beers which are dry-hopped include Exe Valley's Dob's Best Bitter and St Austell's IPA.

Duty

Beer has always been a soft touch for the Exchequer, and duty is a tax levied by the Customs & Excise. At the end of the Second World War, Exeter brewers Norman & Pring worked out that from a pint of mild costing about sixpence, nearly 75 per cent went out in the form of Tax and Excise Duty. Things have improved since.

Price list for Norman & Pring showing their choice of beers – the Customs and Excise must have been rubbing their hands with glee

PRICE LIST.

The City Brewery, EXETER.

IN CASKS.

			Per Gal.
OLD BEER.			
XXX	...	@	1/6
XX	...	,,	1/4
X	...	,,	1/3
MILD ALES.			
Ale ...	...	,,	1/2
A ...	...	,,	1/-
A K	...	,,	10d.
OF A BURTON CHARACTER.			
B B B *Bitter Ale*		,,	1/2
B B	...	,,	1/2
B *Light Dinner Ale.*		,,	1/-
OATMEAL STOUT.			
Most Nutritious		,,	1/2
PORTER.	...	,,	1/-

PRICE LIST.

The City Brewery, EXETER.

IN BOTTLES.

		Per doz. Pints.	Per doz. ½-Pints.
Strong Old Beer	...	—	2/6
Pale Ale ...	...	3/-	1/9
Dinner Ale	...	2/6	1/6
Oatmeal Stout	...	2/6	1/6

All supplied in Screw Stoppered Bottles.

CASES, BOTTLES & STOPPERS WILL BE CHARGED FOR IF NOT RETURNED.

Special Discount allowed to the Trade.

AGENTS APPOINTED.

It is most important that the Beer should not be drawn into a wet jug or glass; the slightest moisture being sufficient to turn the Beer perfectly flat.

E *is for*
Exe and the Exmoor effect...

Ellis Brewery   Hayle, Cornwall

This historic operation started life in 1815 and was based at the Steam Brewery, Brewery Road from 1873. As well as beer, spirits and wine, the brewery was known to have sold wheat, barley, apple, pigs, salt, malt and cheese through its nineteenth-century heyday. In 1934, the brewery merged with Walter Hicks of St Austell and brewing stopped; Ellis' main customers were the workers in the mines, foundries and shipyards of West Cornwall, and when the local economy vanished so did sales of the beer. Hicks renamed the merged operation St Austell, and set up their distribution depot in the Steam Brewery, where it remains to this day. In 2000 an 1872 recipe for one of Ellis' beers was discovered and St Austell's head brewer Roger Ryman used it to make a special one-off ale, Ellis' Original Old Hayle Ale (5.5%). (See **St Austell**.)

Entire

In the early-1700s, one of the most popular beers in London was a blend of three beers. Beer historians suggest that the mix was a strong pale ale from country brewers, London's regular brown ale (apparently a smoky-tasting, murky-looking concoction), and stale beer. Customers would ask for a pint of 'three threads' and the landlord had to do the mix in his own cellar from three barrels. Along came an East End brewer called Harwood who managed to reproduce this style of beer in one barrel, saving landlords the trouble of mixing three beers. This new beer was called Entire, and eventually went on to be called porter. (See **Porter**.)

Esters

Volatile flavour compounds are produced by the work of the yeast on fermenting beer. These esters often produce a fruity (banana/pear) complexity in both aroma and taste.

Exe Valley Brewery   Silverton, Devon

On a clear day you can see Dartmoor from the Exe Valley Brewery. High up on the eastern side of the Exe Valley between Tiverton and

Exe Valley's Guy Sheppard

Conditioning tanks at Exe Valley

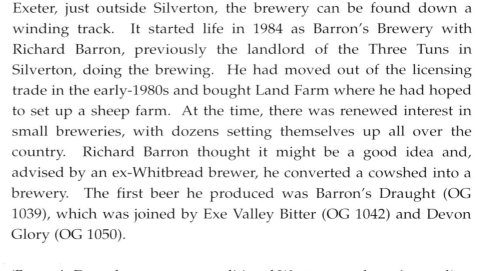

Exeter, just outside Silverton, the brewery can be found down a winding track. It started life in 1984 as Barron's Brewery with Richard Barron, previously the landlord of the Three Tuns in Silverton, doing the brewing. He had moved out of the licensing trade in the early-1980s and bought Land Farm where he had hoped to set up a sheep farm. At the time, there was renewed interest in small breweries, with dozens setting themselves up all over the country. Richard Barron thought it might be a good idea and, advised by an ex-Whitbread brewer, he converted a cowshed into a brewery. The first beer he produced was Barron's Draught (OG 1039), which was joined by Exe Valley Bitter (OG 1042) and Devon Glory (OG 1050).

'Barron's Draught was a very traditional Westcountry brew,' according to Guy Sheppard, who joined forces with Richard Barron in 1991 when Barron's Brewery became the Exe Valley Brewery. Guy, who is originally from the West Midlands, went to Exeter University to read accountancy, but became enamoured of real ale after working at the university bar. On leaving college he set up as an independent beer wholesaling agent. In 1991 he sold the business and joined Richard.

Exe Valley is a 13-barrel brewery, which is well-organised, with different rooms for the various sections of the brewing process. A ladder leads up to the first floor where the malt and hops are kept. 'We are very traditional in our use of hops,' says Guy. Fuggles is used for bittering and Goldings for aroma, while Challenger is used for a bit of both. The tops of the mash tun and copper also protrude into this space from a room which is directly below. Next door are the fermenting vessels. The original brewery space is now the conditioning tank room where beer is pumped from the fermenting vessels after six days, and then kept in tanks for a week or longer. This allows the flavour to deepen and the maturation process to continue. It is all very compact and allows Guy and Richard a great deal of flexibility.

There are six Exe Valley beers available regularly through the year. Exe Valley Bitter is a fruity session beer which is based on Barron's Draught, as Guy explains:

Every brew we have done is adapted from that recipe. Richard spent months perfecting that beer and when he felt it was right relaunched it as Exe Valley Bitter. When I joined, Richard introduced Dob's Best Bitter, which means dry 'op bitter. A local pub wanted a more bitter beer so Richard dry-hopped Exe Valley and drinkers in the pub give it the name Dob's. We've stuck with it and it has become our bestseller. It has also won a few CAMRA awards. So we then took Exe Valley down to 3.7% because we felt we lacked a session bitter.

Other regulars include Barron's Hopsit, Mr Sheppard's Crook and Devon Glory, which is a very malty premium ale, which Guy feels is particularly true to the region's tradition:

It is very West Countryish – very malty, with low hoppiness and an underlying sweetness. There was a lot of that thing in the Westcountry palate with beers such as Starkey's.

The final regular is a dry-hopped strong ale, Exeter Old Bitter, which has also won a fistful of CAMRA awards.

Beers: Exe Valley Bitter (3.7%); Dob's Best Bitter (4.1%); Barron's Hopsit (4.1%); Devon Glory (4.7%); Mr Sheppard's Crook (4.7%); Exeter Old Bitter (4.8%). Occasional: Spring Beer (4.3%); Devon Summer (3.9%); Autumn Glory (4.5%); Winter Glow (6%) and Devon Dawn (4.5%). The mild-style Barron's Dark (4.1%) is occasionally brewed. Bottles: Devon Glory, bottle-conditioned.

Star Beer: Dob's Best Bitter (4.1%) – Amber/light-brown colour with a soft, fruity, citrusy nose which also shows traces of a malty caramel character. On the palate initial maltiness (with a hint of sweetness) is followed by a citrus-influenced fruitiness which continues into the long and bitter finish, which also has some maltiness. A well-balanced fruity bitter.

Recommended outlets: Royal Castle Hotel, Dartmouth; Lamb Inn, Silverton.

Exmoor Ales, Golden Hill Brewery   Wiveliscombe, Somerset

If someone claims to have seen a Stag in this pub, it does not mean the landlord has suddenly decided to set up a nature reserve. Stag is just one of the real ales produced by Exmoor Ales. Located on Golden Hill which overlooks the small town of Wiveliscombe, Exmoor operate from the former loading bay of Hancocks, who brewed in 'Wivvy' until the late-1950s. Brewing returned in 1979 when local man Tim Gilmour-White set up Golden Hill Brewery (Exmoor's original name). The brewery made its mark almost immediately on the beer world by being voted Best Bitter at the prestigious CAMRA Great British Beer Festival in 1980.

A common sight on the roads of the West Country

Since then they have scooped countless other awards. Gilmour-White retired in 1987, and the then head brewer Colin Green and marketing director Jim Laker (who died in 1996) turned to friend Peter Turner and asked him to join them in buying the brewery. This finally happened in August 1988 with Exmoor Ales becoming the official name. The brewery

Exmoor Ales' head brewer Adrian Newman checks out the hops

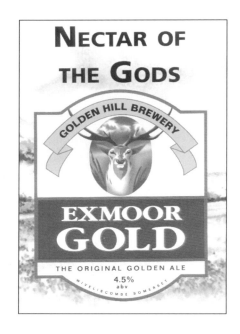

has grown steadily since both in and out of the county, becoming one of the UK's most successful small breweries. Currently, there are 12 full-time staff, and 45 barrels can be produced in one go which they are able to do 14 times a week – that is a lot of beer!

Peter Turner and head brewer Adrian Newman (he joined in 1992) are currently the sole directors of the company. Like many brewers, Adrian Newman was a teenage home-brewer who made a business of his hobby. 'I was fourteen years old and making stuff that was 7%,' he recalls. After graduating from Heriot-Watt with a degree in brewing, he went on to work at long-established Scottish brewers Belhaven, in Dunbar. He was there for ten years, learning all about the business of brewing, until he was tempted south by Exmoor.

As for raw materials, malt comes from Tuckers Maltings. Hops are mainly English (Goldings, Fuggles, Challenger), though ones from the Czech Republic and Germany are used. The beers Adrian Newman has nurtured and developed over the last ten years reflect his belief that a well-balanced beer is what drinkers want.

Our beers aren't incredibly hoppy. There are lots more bitter beers, but ours are very well balanced. The secret of our success is the drinkability of the beers.

Exmoor produces five regular beers, with four other seasonal ones released during the year. As already mentioned, many of the names reflect the wildlife of the area: Fox, Hart, Stag and Beast. Exmoor Ale, the beer which scooped the first award all those years ago, remains a wonderful session beer with its initial maltiness giving way to the bite and snap of a hoppy finish. Other regulars are Fox with its subtle maltiness and long, bitter-sweet finish, the original 'Golden Ale' Exmoor Gold, and Stag. This is a full-bodied warming ale, originally specially brewed for Somerset Cricket Club. Too many of these and you are definitely out for a duck.

Beers: Ale (3.8%); Fox (4.2%); Gold (4.5%); Hart (4.8%); Stag (5.2%). Seasonal: Hound Dog (4%); Wild Cat (4.4%); Exmas (5%); Beast (6.6%). Bottles: Gold; Beast.

Recommended outlets: London Inn, Molland; Sportsmans Inn, Sandyway, South Molton.

Star Beer: Stag (5.2%) – Chestnut-brown colour, with a resiny hop nose mingling with the grainy biscuityness of malt. A full-bodied strong ale with well-defined fruitiness on the palate which is more than matched by the chewy maltiness. A very well-balanced and warming ale which is strong but deceptively moreish.

F *is for*
flavour, firkins and Fizgigs...

Firkin

Brewing name given to a nine-gallon cask. After that, casks double in size, an 18-gallon one being called a kilderkin, and the rarely used hogshead holding 36 gallons. The vanished puncheon and butt held 72 and 108 gallons respectively. The butt gave us the word buttery, as found in some old colleges. At the bottom end of the scale a pin is a small 4.5-gallon cask.

Fizgig & Firkin   Exeter, Devon

Brew-pub which was part of the Firkin Brewery pub chain. The building which housed the Fizgig & Firkin was originally on the site of the bottling hall/store of the St Anne's Well Brewery, and during the early-1990s it was converted into a pub called the St Anne's Well Brewery. According to one seasoned observer of the Exeter pub scene, it was one of the best pubs in the city for real ale. In the mid-1990s the pub was leased to the Firkin chain and brewing started up for a brief time until its demise in 1999 and relaunch as the Fizgig. This in turn was shut down in late-2001, apparently owing to complaints about the noise from live bands.

Flavour

What does beer taste of? What we taste when drinking beer comes from the malt and hops used; esters also add something to the flavour of some beers, as does the action of the yeast. The tongue recognises sweetness at the front, saltiness and sourness in the middle, while bitterness comes in at the back. That is why we talk of a bitter finish to a beer. Maltiness is recognised by its cereal, biscuity, nutty, coffee bean, chocolate or vinous fruits qualities, depending on what types of malt are used. This usually makes itself known at the beginning of the tasting; malt character can also be present in the finish. Malt also gives dryness. Various hops offer fruity, citrusy, peppery, spicy, resiny, tangy, zesty or earthy qualities. We want balance in the flavour of a beer. Too much maltiness and it becomes cloying and sticky, too much hop bitterness and it sears the palate, making for a stern and austere beer. The magic of brewing is to create a beer with a flavour that the palate wants more of. In recent years, brewers have widened the boundaries of what we regard as the flavour of beer with the use of fruit, smoked malts, honey and spices. These are not modern gimmicks, but often rediscoveries. The easiest answer to the question: what does beer taste of? A lot. (See **Tasting**.)

Fruity stuff: Sutton Brewery's Orangatang

Fruit Beer

Many people might blanch at the thought of a fruit-flavoured beer but several Belgian beer classics are lambic beers made with either cherry or raspberry, while British brewers have been adding fruit to their beers for some years now. Over here fruit is usually added during the boil, so that the flavour is not too overpowering. In the West Country, fruit beers are few and far between, but Sutton in Plymouth occasionally make an orange beer which uses the peel and juice in the boil, Orangatang (4.4%). 'A good summer beer,' says head brewer Ben Ridgeon.

Furgusons Brewery in Plympton, sadly now closed

Furgusons   Plympton, Devon

Brewing conglomerate Allied set up this brewery in the Devon depot of another one of their breweries, Halls. By the early-1990s, Furgusons was brewing three real ales which were going out to Allied pubs in the area plus the free trade. The three were Dartmoor Best Bitter (3.7%), Dartmoor Strong (4.5%) and Cockleroaster (6.5%). By the mid-1990s, Allied had merged with Carlsberg-Tetley, and Furgusons became Plympton Brewery. Not long afterwards the inevitable rationalisation meant the closure of the brewery, with the three beers being contract-brewed by St Austell. Nowadays, Dartmoor Best Bitter is the only beer to have survived. Still brewed by St Austell, and upped in strength to 3.9%, it can be found throughout the West Country.

Beers produced by Furgusons at their Plympton plant

G *is for*
glug, glass and gravity...

Glassware

In Ireland if you ask for a glass of beer, you are given a half-pint. In this country we ask for halves or pints, which are usually served in straight glasses, or a 'sleeve'. Some pubs, especially in the West Country, offer handled dimpled mugs, which are also called 'handles' or 'jugs'. Serious drinkers prefer these, because by holding on to the handle they can avoid their hands warming up the precious ale. Some breweries produce special pint glasses with their name or logo engraved on them (Otter Brewery have a particularly handsome example), while a great number of CAMRA beer festivals produce special commemorative glasses which a few people (mainly men much to their partners' dismay) collect. Sadly, or not if you are a licensee, British drinkers have declined to go down the route of Belgian beers, where there is a glass for every beer. It can be argued that distinctive glasses for various beer styles such as barley wine, best bitter, mild and wheat beer, would lift beer's image, and make it more food- and female-friendly.

Greenslade's St Mary's Church Brewery at Torquay in 1985

Gravity

Term given to a method of serving beer, where it is served straight from cask, usually situated behind the bar. A few pubs still serve their beers this way, with casks usually found at the back of the bar wearing a cooling jacket. Gravity also refers to the density of the beer. (See **Original Gravity**.)

Green beer

Name given to beer which has gone through its first fermentation in the brewery, but has not spent enough time in cask during secondary fermentation to enable rough and unhewn flavours to be matured out. It is always unpleasant to drink.

Greenslade Brothers   Torquay, Devon

Set up in the mid-1850s at Fore Street, round the back of the Palk Arms, this originally was called the Palk Arms Brewery. Brewer David Green boasted that his beers were similar to those of Burton, because he got

Stone jug from Greenslade Bros

his brewing liquor from a spring with 'peculiar' qualities. Apparently, brewing analysts tested the waters and agreed with him. John Greenslade became the next owner, and by 1880 the brewery changed its name to Greenslade Brothers, and had also set itself up as a wine merchants. This was common practice for many brewers and it survives to this day, with St Austell having a separate wines and spirits division. One of Greenslade's more popular beers was called Eclipse Stout, named after their sales slogan 'Prize medal ales which "eclipsed" all'. Brewing came to an end in 1927, a couple of years after Plymouth Breweries took over the business.

Guest Beer

Most pubs have their regular ales, which are available all the time. Guest beers are those which turn up for a short period and are chosen from a variety of breweries. For that reason, pubs with a constant rotation of guest beers are always popular with the more obsessive beer fans (who are sometimes called tickers or scoopers), as it often allows them to taste beers from all over the country. Westcountry pubs with a high turnover of guest beers include the Blisland Inn, Blisland, the Star Inn at Crowlas, and the Great Western Hotel, Exeter.

H *is for*
hops, health and hauntings...

Handpumps

When a pub boasts handles which the barperson pulls to draw beer up from the cask, it is a visible sign that real ale is available. Up until the end of the eighteenth century, beer was served straight from cask to mug or jug. Things changed when Thomas Parkinson developed a hydrostatic engine or machine which could draw beer from a pub's cellar. It was called the leather bucket machine and the first step towards the handpump. The introduction of the handpump (also called handpull) enabled landlords to keep their casks in cellars, where temperatures were much kinder to the beer.

Harvest Ale

One of the more welcome aspects of the revival of seasonal ales is the appearance of harvest beers, with their use of fresh green hops (hops are normally dried in a kiln to preserve them), which is called 'green-hopping'. Obviously this only happens after the harvest, but it makes for a dry, highly-hopped thirst-quencher which is very welcome as the summer often lingers on into early autumn. Hop experts also say that the effect of green hops is rather like using fresh herbs in cooking, with more fragrant flavours being produced. It is a rare style in the West Country, with Cotleigh's Harvest Ale being the most regular year after year. However, Skinner's brewed a one-off Green Hop Ale in 2001, with Golding hops being sent straight to the brewery without under-going the normal drying process. This produced what Steve Skinner called 'the Beaujolais Nouveau of beers'. There also used to be an undistinguished beer called Harvest which was brewed all year round in Burton upon Trent for Allied Breweries' pubs in the West Country.

Haunted Pubs

Old buildings seem to attract ghosts, and many of the ancient inns of the West Country are no exception. Noted sightings have included the Bishop Lacey at Chudleigh, where several regulars apparently saw a handpump pull a pint of beer on its own, and the Northmore Arms at Wonson, haunted by the apparition of a mutton-chop whiskered old

Tally Ho's regular beer Nutters, with an unusual pumpclip attached to its handpump

seadog. Other pubs reputedly visited by spirits not out of an optic are the Fisherman's Cott, Bickleigh, and the Kingsbridge Inn at Totnes. On a less serious note, one regular at the unhaunted Blisland Inn on Bodmin Moor has been known to commune with his long-dead father by pouring a pint of beer on his grave!

Head

The collar of foam on the top of a pint of beer, also known as top, is a serious issue for the dedicated drinker. In the North of England drinkers like a thick and smooth creamy head which is produced by pulling the beer through a showercap-like nozzle attached to the pump. This is called a sparkler. Drinkers in the south have always gone for a flatter, thinner head which usually breaks up as the pint goes down. The success of the new generation of keg beers such as Caffrey's and John Smith's Smooth, with their inch of shaving foam on top, have led to an increased use of sparklers on beers in some Westcountry hostelries. Some brewers and publicans believe that drawing a beer through a sparkler helps the appearance, whilst others think it, 'takes the guts out of a beer,' as one landlord succinctly puts it.

Head first: O'Hanlon's beer showing off their foamy heads, with Red Ale left, then wheat beer, Organic rye and Port Stout

Health and Beer

Beer is good for you – in moderation, containing no fat or cholesterol and fewer calories than the same volume of milk. It also has dietary fibre, and the alcohol content is linked to a reduction in cardio-vascular disease if taken in moderation, usually two pints a day. Beer is also rich in silicon, which helps to increase bone density, the decrease of which is connected with osteoporosis.

Heavitree Brewing Company   Exeter, Devon

The last brewery to operate in Exeter started off as Wilcocks & Rewe, but in the *Billings Directory & Gazetteer* of the County of Devon in 1857 it is noted as Heavitree Brewery with one Elizabeth Baker as brewer. Brewing at the Church Street site came to an end in 1970 when the directors cited mounting costs and a change of public taste as the main reasons for the decision. 'We are giving the public what it wants and streamlining for the future,' said its managing director at the time, WP Tucker. Brewing had been in decline for several years with only 45 per cent of the company's 135 pubs taking Heavitree beers, which included a light ale, brown ale, 3X mild, draft bitter and a strong ale IPA bitter. Heavitree still retains a pub estate of 112 pubs, most of which are found in Devon.

Honey

Honey has been used to give flavour to alcoholic drinks for many centuries – the remains of a Bronze Age beaker from 3000BC Scotland was found to contain a type of honey which could have been used for mead. It was also used in beer and ale for centuries, and has enjoyed a comeback in the last few years. The simple sugars of honey help fermentation and boost alcohol; honey also offsets some of the bitterness of hops, letting their floral qualities shine through. Too much, though, and it can be cloying and ruin the beer. Honey can be added prior to fermentation or in the cask. For a taste of a Westcountry honey beer, try Skinner's Heligan Honey Restoration Ale.

Star Beer: Heligan Honey Restoration Ale (4%) – Dark-gold in colour. An attractive, flowery, hoppy nose leads the charge with hints of dark malt (almost slightly chocolatey) and honey in the background. On the palate, there is a good malty start before a delicious fruitiness kicks in, leading to a bitter finish. There is also the subtle flavour of honey somewhere in the finish, which helps to balance the bitterness.

Skinner's Brewery, with head brewer Will Freeland, who uses honey to give a buzz to one of his beers

Hops

Along with malt, yeast and liquor (water), the humble hop is all that is needed to make good beer. While barley provides the malt sugars for the yeast to convert into alcohol, hops provide bitterness, aroma and preservative qualities; a counterbalance to the sweetness and biscuity quality of the malt. Hop cones contain a sticky yellow powder called lupulin; it is from this that resins and oils are produced. The resins are a source of bitterness and preservative qualities, while the oils provide flavour and aroma. Some hops, which are high in alpha acids, are used to provide bitterness, while others are used for aroma. They are added to the brew in the shape of dried cones, pellets and occasionally as hop oil, though aficionados frown on the use of the latter. Fresh hops are occasionally used just after the harvest to produce a spicy, fresh-tasting beer in a process called 'green-hopping'. One of the skills of the brewer is to pick the hops which will work together and then use the right quantities; in recent years there has been a trend for single-varietal hop beers, bringing out the best from the hop used.

Above: *John Lawton, Teignworthy Brewery, in the hop store*
Above right: *Hopping mad: the hop collection at Scattor Rock*

It is hard to imagine beer brewed without hops, but up until the 1500s, the main drink of the British Isles was 'ale', a strong sweet brew of malted barley flavoured with spices, herbs and bark of trees. 'Beer', by comparison, was a foreign concoction, a hopped beverage drunk by Flems, Germans and the Dutch. The first recorded instance of hopped beer arriving on these shores has been traced back to the early-1400s, with a shipment destined for Dutch merchants working here. In 1450, the presence of hops in beer was blamed for stirring up the rebellion of Jack Cade in Kent. Even though Henry VIII tried to outlaw beer by banning the use of hops in brewing, by the mid-1550s ale was compared with beer and found wanting... 'Thick and fulsome, and no longer popular except with a few'. Hopped beer had become the dominant drink and ale never reclaimed its place.

In the late-eighteenth century, the famous Goldings hop was developed, and 100 years later Fuggles was introduced to the world. Goldings and Fuggles became the two main hops for English bitter, both being unusually low in the alpha acids which give bitterness to beer. The former gives off rich, resiny, citrusy aromas and flavours; the latter has a well-rounded bitterness and is often used as a gentle bittering hop. These days brewers are experimenting with all sorts of hops. Some are looking to American varieties with their aromatic qualities (Bideford's Jollyboat for instance). There are also organic hops, most of which are brought in from abroad. Each variety has different qualities. As well as Fuggles and Goldings, other hops used include Challenger (bittering hop, lemony and peppery); Target (bittering hop, resiny, floral); First Gold (aromatic, tangerine); Brambling Cross (blackcurrant); Phoenix (bittering hop, citrusy, fruitiness); Northdown (bittering hop, full fruitiness); Hallertau (flowery, used for lagers); Williamette (slightly fruity and spicy); and Cascade (perfumey, lychee, muscat). (See **Aroma Hop, Brewing, Bittering Hop, Dry-Hopping, Late Hops.**)

HSD

Legendary strong ale from St Austell Brewery with an ABV of 5%. It was introduced in 1975, selling for 26p a pint. The initials stand for Hicks Special Draught, but Westcountry wags have coined other names – Hicks' Sudden Death and High Speed Diesel. (See **St Austell.**)

The legendary St Austell strong beer, HSD

I *is for*
inn, IPA (and imbibe)...

Imperial Porter or Stout

After the emergence of porter in the eighteenth century, the strongest were called stout porters, which evolved into today's stouts. As the British Empire expanded, some of the porters were also brewed for export. These had to be strong enough to survive the journey on the high seas, and were heavily hopped to help resist infection, and the alcohol strength was higher; this kept the beers for much longer. The exported brews were called imperial porters or stouts, or Russian stouts, and were especially popular in that country and the Baltic before the Revolution. Courage's Imperial Russian Stout was a classic example of this robust style until it was discontinued in the 1990s, but the West Country has an excellent example with Edwin Tucker's Empress Russian Porter produced by Teignworthy. (**See Porter, Stout, Teignworthy.**)

Star Beer: Edwin Tucker's Empress Russian Porter (10.5%) – This bottle-conditioned ale is produced annually and matures for some years. It is very dark, almost black in colour with a cappuccino-coloured head. On the nose there is a fruitiness which suggests fresh dessert apples, with maltiness, alcohol and a suggestion of hop in the background. The palate includes caramel, fruit, fruit cake, treacle, toffee, malt, followed by an intense and lingering hoppy bitterness. As the beer warms up there are some hints of vanilla on the palate; it has a very bitter and spicy finish.

Inn

Traditionally this was a licensed premises whose main clientele were travellers. Nowadays it is an interchangeable term depending on the licensee's pretensions. Usually, though, when we think of modern inns, we think of rural pubs which offer good food and accommodation. Or as Dr Johnson put it:

There is nothing which has yet been contrived by man, by which so much happiness is produced as by a good tavern or inn.

The London Inn, Molland, on Exmoor, one of many Westcountry inns which offer good food and beer

IPA

This is otherwise known as India Pale Ale after the highly hopped, strong-in-alcohol, pale-coloured ales which were sent out to India in the early years of the nineteenth century. Before then, beer on the long passage to India spoilt easily and was undrinkable. Hops and alcohol helped with preservation, while the length of passage meant that there was enough time for fermentation to smooth out the rough edges. One London brewer, Hodgson, cornered the market for IPAs but he also managed to upset the imperial powers-that-be, with the result that they passed on a bottle of his beer to several Burton brewers and asked them to produce a similar beer. Legend has it that one of the Burton brewers managed to use his teapot to clone Hodgson's IPA. Once Burton upon Trent got in on the act, the IPA style of beer became indelibly associated with the town.

It also became a popular drink throughout the UK when a ship carrying a cargo of IPA destined for India was shipwrecked off Liverpool in 1827. The salvaged barrels were sold in and around Liverpool, and its fame spread, a process which was considerably helped by the development of the railway network. For the next few decades, IPA was the fashionable beer of the middle classes, who wanted something different from the dark, murky porters and stouts beloved of the working classes. By the 1880s, however, IPA's strength was seen as a disadvantage and weaker pale ales entered the market. This eventually led to the emergence of bitter and pale ale. During the twentieth century, IPA has become a misleading, catch-all phrase for pale beers, many of which are much weaker than the original Victorian style. In the West Country, Edwin Tucker's East India Pale Ale (6.5%), produced by Teignworthy, is an excellent recreated true IPA. (See **Bitter, Pale Ale, Teignworthy**.)

Star Beer: Edwin Tucker's East India Pale Ale (6.5%) – A light-coloured ale, with a strong hoppy nose which is reminiscent of Seville oranges; there is also a hint of malt in the background. On the palate the hoppy, citrus notes dominate, followed by a satisfyingly bitter finish. As the beer warms up in the glass a fruitiness (lime marmalade) also make its presence felt. Tuckers Maltings specially kilned a separate batch of East India Malt for this limited edition ale, and had the beer brewed to a recipe from the 1870s.

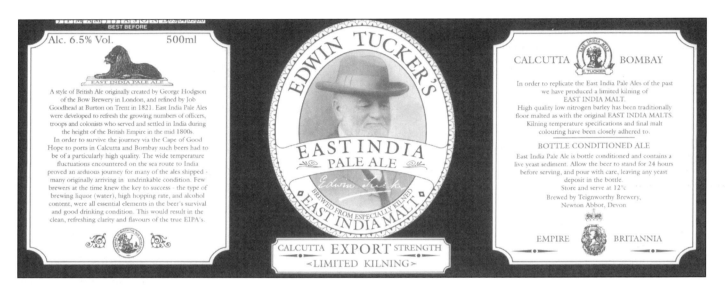

J *is for*
jugs and jollyboats...

Jollyboat Brewery   Bideford, Devon

The last time the port of Bideford was home to its own brewery was in the 1920s, when three were recorded during the year of the General Strike. This was followed by a drought until 1995, when former town planner and keen home-brewer Hugh Parry and his son Simon started up Jollyboat Brewery. It was based in the coach-house of a classical early-nineteenth-century house which used to belong to a surgeon. 'We lived in the flat above,' Hugh remembers, 'and the garage below became vacant. It seemed like a good idea to set up a brewery.'

It is a five-barrel operation, with Hugh now doing the brewing on his own. He brews twice a week, using a much-travelled mash tun, which came to him via the long-defunct Nailsea Brewery in Bristol and the still thriving Wychwood. Even though the brewery seems rather tight for space, he says he has room to expand and could brew three times as much such is the demand for his gorgeously and well-crafted fruity beers. Hops are a mixture of Fuggles and Goldings, but he also makes use of the aromatic American hop Cascade. 'I tend to do one hop beers,' says Hugh, who adds that the sort of beers he personally likes are 'dry bitter ones, but I daren't do beers like that or they wouldn't sell.' Mainbrace and Freebooter are his regulars, while others include the award-winning session ale Buccaneers, which usually comes out in

A lifebelt at the Jollyboat Brewery reflects the nautical names of the beers

Below left: *Jollyboat Brewery, with brewer Hugh Parry*
Below: *The mash tun at Jollyboat with the mash inside*

the summer, plus stronger beers Privateer, Plunder and Christmas Contraband, the latter described as a festive porter for Christmas. In 2002 a new beer, Corsair, was introduced, which breaks Hugh's hop rules in that both Fuggles and Goldings are used. 'I'm still developing its flavour,' Hugh says. 'It is a premium mid-brown bitter. There is also a little bit of chocolate malt which gives it a slightly Caribbean touch.'

As might be guessed from the nautical names of his beers, Hugh is keen on the sea; living in Bideford it would hard to ignore. 'All people involved in the brewery are interested in sailing,' he says. And the name of the brewery? Apparently, a jollyboat was perhaps one of a sailor's most favourite vessels. In the days of sailing ships it was the name given to the vessel which took the crew of a ship ashore for a welcome spell in the tavern after they had spent many a month on the high seas.

Beers: Freebooter (4%); Mainbrace (4.2%); Corsair (4.5%). Occasional: Buccaneer (3.7%); Plunder (4.8%); Privateer (4.8%); Christmas Contraband (5.8%). Bottles: Privateer, bottle-conditioned.

Star Beer: Mainbrace (4.2%) – Dark-golden best bitter, with a lemony, fruity nose. Biscuity malt provides the introduction on the palate, before a citrusy fruitiness balances any movement towards over-maltiness. The finish is bitter, hoppy and dry with some lingering fruitiness. There is also a slight amount of sweetness on the finish. A mid-strength bitter with plenty of fruity hop character.

Recommended pubs: Bridge Inn, Topsham; George Hotel, South Molton.

Jug and Bottle

This was the old name given to the part of the pub where people could buy beer to drink at home. It was usually sold in jugs brought in by the customer, special stoneware flagons produced by the pub, and later on in bottles. You can occasionally see pubs, usually built in the early-twentieth century or before, with the words Jug and Bottle etched in stone above the former off-sales' entrance. Nowadays, some pubs, especially brew-pubs such as the Beer Engine, have plastic half-gallon jugs for drinkers to take the beer home.

K *is for*
keg, Keltek and Kripple Dick!...

Keg

This somewhat unoriginal nickname refers to keg beer, which the big breweries foisted on the drinking public from the 1950s onwards. Ironically, such tactics also sparked off the real ale drinkers' revolt in the shape of CAMRA. Keg was the complete antithesis of real cask-conditioned ale, as it did not undergo a secondary fermentation – it was not a living product. It was pasteurised, gassed up, chilled and could be kept in a keg for a long time. Landlords did not need to worry about tapping and spiling and all the other tasks which keep an ale fresh. Lots of money was flung at keg beer and some of the ad campaigns are still remembered today. Most scorn is reserved for Watney's Red Barrel which became the very devil to real ale drinkers. The likes of CAMRA and their supporters in the media also made the point that keg beer was not much stronger than a cup of tea, while others complained that the excessive gassiness and fizz was hardly conducive to digestion. There are still plenty of keg beers around, but these days they are marketed as nitro-keg or smoothflow, which follow the fashion for beers with creamy foamy heads. They are still cold and gassy, and taste of nothing much. (See **CAMRA, Nitro-keg, Real Ale**.)

John Kelland   Kingsbridge, Devon

Brewery set up in the mid-1850s, with William Kelland taking it over in 1872. Several years later his brother John was in control and the brewery moved from Ebrington Street to Church Street in Kingsbridge. John Kelland also operated as a maltster and hop dealer, and the brewery ran 11 tied houses. However, 1904 saw the whole business put up for auction, and it was bought by Bedford Brewery of Plymouth.

Keltek Brewing Company   Lostwithiel, Cornwall

Back in the late-1940s Andy White's father went to St Austell Brewery to help install some new equipment. In the middle of the job, he received a call to say that his wife had delivered their baby safe and sound, and he went back home to Essex to see his newborn son. Nearly fifty years later the family connection to beer, brewing and Cornwall is

Above: *Keltek Brewery with fermenting vessels to the left and the mash tun to the right*
Above right: *Andy White in the Keltek Brewery, with another batch of bottle beers*

restored with Keltek Brewery, run by Andy White in the ancient stannary town of Lostwithiel. Formed in 1995 by Stuart Heath near Truro, it moved to its current home on an industrial estate at the end of 1998. Stuart still owns the two-and-a-half-barrel kit, but it is Andy who brews the beers.

'I've always had a passion for beer,' admits Andy, who was a home-brewer once upon a time. He was also a captain in the Merchant Navy, and after stepping ashore he moved down to the West Country where his family had a holiday-camp business. His job was to organise getting the beers in from wholesalers. Eventually, he set up as a wholesaler on his own near Bodmin in 1985, before selling out ten years later and going to work for another company. A couple of years later he was on his own again and not long afterwards became involved with Keltek. 'I look for well-balanced beers,' he says. 'They tend to be on the citrusy side.' Hops used are Hallertau, Cascade, First Gold and Challenger, varieties which give flowery and perfumed aromas and

fruity flavours. They are certainly popular and have won several awards.

Andy is a busy man. Not only does he brew, but he also bottles some of Keltek's beers, as well as those of at least a dozen other Westcountry concerns, including Blackawton, Summerskills and Sutton. This started when Stuart bought some bottling equipment after Andy said he would bottle Keltek King. He recalls:

I had three bottles left, and stuck them in the Tuckers Maltings bottled beer competition. Much to my surprise I won. Then I started asking other breweries if they wanted their beers bottled.

Then there is the beer wholesaling business which sees him out on the road many days of the week. Yet, amazingly, despite all this diversification, Keltek has a wide range of beers, going from the golden-coloured session beer Golden Lance to a stupefying barley wine, Kripple Dick (another St Austell connection). There is also another set of beers which appears under the name of Castle Brewery (named after nearby Castle Restormel which was built for the Black Prince), again with a wide range of strengths. Thanks to Andy's energy and efforts there are at least 50 pubs in Cornwall and North Devon which take his beers and the sight of those colourful, quasi-mystical pumpclips at the bar is always a sign of good beer.

Beers: Keltek: 4K Mild (3.8%); Golden Lance (3.8%); Cross (3.8%); Magik (4.2%); King (5.1%). Occasional: Smugglers (4.2%); Pirates (4.8%); Revenge (7%); Kripple Dick (8.5%). **Castle Brewery:** Roundhead (3.6%); Jousters Bitter (4%); Execution Ale (4.2%); Prince of Ales (4.5%); Legend (4.8%). Occasional: Myth (4.2%); Once A Knight (5.1%); Lostwithiale (7%); Black Prince (8.5%). Bottles: King; Revenge; Kripple Dick, all bottle-conditioned.

Star Beer: Revenge (7%) – Very dark-brown in colour with reddish tints. An enticing nose with dried fruit, rich fruit cake and hints of baked banana jostling to emerge. On the palate there is some biscuity malt before a full fruity mid-palate which is reminiscent of berry fruit; it is also wine-like on the palate. The finish is bittersweet and dry with fruit and malt also hanging around. Beware this beer – it is easy to drink, despite its strength.

Recommended outlets: Royal Oak, Lostwithiel; Rashleigh Arms, Polkerris.

King's Head Brewery and Ale House   Plymouth, Devon

Landlord Neil Potts opened this small brewery in the back of his pub, one of the oldest in Plymouth, at the beginning of 1994. King's Ransom

(4%) was the first beer out of the mash, with others following including Bretonside Best (4.2%), Gez's Ale (5%), Golden Goose (5%), Ma Husson's Strong Ale (5.6%) and Old Hoppy (5.6%). Business was good and beers went out to other outlets as well as the Little Mutton Monster pub which was also owned by Potts. Unfortunately, the pub was put on the market in 1996 and brewing came to an end when it was sold a year or so later.

L *is for*
local, lager and last orders...

Labologist

The title by which serious-minded beer label collectors call themselves. In 1959, the Labologists' Society started up, inspired by a Guinness promotion campaign involving beer labels. However, the practice of beer label collecting goes back much further. During the First World War, servicemen who were being shunted around the country kept collections of beer labels from all the breweries in the areas in which they were stationed. This was their way of keeping a record of where they had been because they were not allowed to have diaries, and most breweries in those days were very local. Beer labels these days are colourful, evocative and informative about the beer you are about to drink. Sometimes we are even told the history of the beer in a few words. It was not always so – at one stage labels rarely mentioned the alcoholic strength or the ingredients.

Every label tells a story: Teignworthy Brewery's Millennium Ale

Above: *St Austell's Brown Willy Ale*
Above right: *St Austell Cornish Ale produced for Jamaica Inn*

Lacework

The name given to the intricate patterns that the head of the beer makes on the inside of the glass as it is drunk. The lack of lacework with a pint sometimes means that the beer has passed its best, even though it is still drinking OK.

Lager

Lager was first brewed in these isles in the 1880s when breweries in Wales and Scotland thought that there might be a market for the golden beers of central Europe. Over the years lager was seen as a specialist drink, a thirst-quencher to be drunk by John Mills and his chums in *Ice Cold In Alex*, or 'one for the ladies' as suggested by Andrew Campbell in his *Book of Beer*, published in the mid-1950s. However, in the 1960s and 70s, lager really took off as aggressive and inventive TV advertising influenced newly affluent drinkers, persuading them that this was the beverage for 'now'. These British-brewed lagers were weak in alcohol and heavily carbonated, but they increased their market share at the expense of bitter.

However, for all the brand recognition of the word lager, if you went into a bierkeller in Germany and asked for one, you would be met with a puzzled look. Lager in German means storeroom. The long conditioning time of German beers is called lagering. Over in Germany and Central Europe, lagered beers come in a variety of styles: Marzens, Bocks, Festbiers, Pilsners, Oktoberbiers, Helles, Budvars and Dortmunds. A real lager is a wonderful beer with a fresh, spritzy and rounded palate of soft malt and a gentle hoppy, bitter finish, though the North-German Jever Pils has an uncommonly ferocious bitter finish. The fermentation process for lager is unique. Lagers undergo bottom-fermentation, in which all the yeast goes to the bottom and works in a much cooler temperature than ale yeast. Once the first fermentation is completed, lager beers are put into conditioning tanks (or lagering tanks) where a full attenuation can take place over a few weeks, though many cost-conscious companies have cut that time. Attenuation is a process whereby all the malt sugars left are turned into carbon dioxide and alcohol, giving the lager a smooth, soft character.

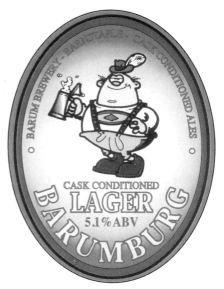

Local lager: Barum Brewery's Barumburg

A few years ago, the very word lager would have been enough to send ale aficionados back behind their pint to utter curses against the fizzy, ice-cold amber nectar. However, even though lager still maintains its massive lead in the market, what we mean by lager has broadened out greatly in the past few years. Many drinkers have had their eyes opened by the wider availability of traditional Czech Pilsners such as Pilsner Urquell (4.4%) and Budvar (5%). Then there have been the small micro-breweries, usually noted for their ales, which have started making lagers. These beers may not be truly authentic, and the hoppiness is more apparent than in a real lager, but they have convinced some real ale drinkers that there is more to lager than straw-coloured firewater for youngsters. Westcountry breweries making good lager-style beers include Barum (Barumburg, 5.1%), Branscombe Vale (Horn Lager, 4.7%), Otter (Bright, 4.3%), Scattor Rock (Scat Tor Rockin' Lager, 4.6%) and Teignworthy (Beachcomber, 4.7%).

Star Beer: Otter Bright (4.3%) – Strictly speaking, this is a golden beer rather than a lager, but because Otter Brewery uses bottom-fermenting yeast for all its beers, and lager and wheat malt make up the grist, this is the sort of beer which appeals to lager drinkers. Patrick McCaig at the brewery admitted as much, explaining, 'Otter Bright is a tool to get the young drinking beer.' Pale in colour, it has a soft, malty nose with some hop in the background; on the palate there is a well-rounded malt character, a good fruitiness and a long finish with plenty of hoppiness. It is very thirst-quenching and an excellent ale and lager hybrid.

Lakeman's   Brixham, Devon

Started in 1780, this long-established brewery stayed with the Lakeman family until 1901. It was then sold, but brewing continued under the Lakeman's name. Simonds took over in 1937, taking control of the 50 tied houses, before closing the business in 1950.

Last Orders…

…The worst sound in the world for the dedicated pub-goer is the traditional call of the licensee when he wants you out of his pub. Usually called at 10.50pm, this is followed by drinking up time which is twenty minutes from 11pm. It used to be ten minutes which led to scenes where two pints were downed in record time. Licensees use different methods in trying to get you out. Some walk amongst drinkers, collecting glasses and politely telling them they have to close, but others bellow out as if they were on the parade ground. The very bellicose shout such classics as, 'haven't you lot got homes to go to', or stand over the hapless remaining drinker as they try to drain your pint. There have been calls for Britain's nannyish licensing laws to be brought into line with that of Europe's. Until then, keep your eye on the clock as it approaches 10.50pm.

Late Hops

These are aroma hops which are added late in the boil. They are low in alpha acid and designed to add to the aromatic qualities of the finished beer. (See **Brewing, Hops**.)

John Leggett   Teignmouth

Brew-pub based at the Half Moon Hotel on Holland's Row during the nineteenth century. John Leggett became landlord and brewer in 1878, serving customers and making beer until 1910, when the brewery closed.

Licensing Hours

The period of time in which a public house is legally allowed to sell alcohol has been a contentious issue stretching back for centuries. The state has always had a say as to when taverns, inns and public houses can pull their pints. In the Middle Ages, London taverns had to shut their doors when curfew was called, as these establishments were seen as hiding places for thieves. During the nineteenth century, beer could legally be sold from early in the morning until late at night. In the First World War Lloyd George declared war on the drinking habits of the nation, and proclaimed, 'We are fighting Germany, Austria and drink and the greatest of those foes is drink.' As a result, pubs' opening hours were shortened (a law which was not changed until very recently), with pubs usually opening from 11am–3pm during the day and 5.30pm, or even later, to 11pm. Sunday hours, as many drinkers will recall, were even shorter. This all changed in 1988 with the introduction of all-day opening in England and Wales, to be followed by Sunday-afternoon opening in 1995. There has been a continuing debate about 24-hour opening ever since, though the early opening times permitted in the World Cup 2002 suggests that 'open all hours' could be here sooner rather than later.

Light Ale
Low-alcohol bottled beer which was traditionally one half of that old favourite light and bitter. (See **Pale Ale**.)

Local
Long-established nickname for the pub just round the corner, where a drinker goes regularly. In the 1960s, a series of TV adverts publicising the pub featured celebrities of the day 'down at the local'. Stars appearing included the World Cup winning players Bobby Moore and Martin Peters. The mind boggles at the thought of Michael Owen and David Beckham doing a similar thing today.

Lundy Brewery
(See **Marisco Tavern Brewery**.)

M *is for*
malt, mild and milk stout...

Malt

Malt is known in brewing lore as the soul of beer; without it there can be no beer. When barley is malted, it undergoes a process of part-germination which activates enzymes so they are ready to convert starch into fermentable sugars on which yeast will feed and turn into alcohol during fermentation. As well as flavour and aroma, malt gives beer its distinctive palate of colours. A golden ale sparkling in the sunlight of a beer garden will have been made solely with a pale malt, which has a biscuity flavour if crunched before being milled for the grist – pale is the main malt used in a brew because it has the highest levels of starch and the enzymes which convert starch into fermentable sugars. Others are used in smaller quantities. An amber colour means that a pinch of crystal malt, with its toffee and nutty savour, has been added to give body and flavour. Dark stouts and porters are achieved by the addition of dark malts, highly roasted grains which produce tastes such as chocolate, fruit cake and espresso coffee. There is also roasted barley, which gives the likes of Guinness that distinctive burnt edge; this is barley which has been roasted but not malted. Maris Otter malt, one of several strains available to the brewer, is generally regarded as the Rolls-Royce of malts, despite its premium price. (See **Brewing**.)

Above: *Two of a kind: chocolate malt* (left) *and pale malt*
Right: *St Austell's malt store*

Before beer, there is malt as this scene at Tuckers Maltings shows

Maltings

A maltings, or malt-house, is where barley is malted in preparation for its eventual conversion into a pint of beer. In the nineteenth century malt-houses were common sights in the towns of the West Country, but today Tuckers Maltings in Newton is the only one in the West Country using the traditional floor-malted method of production.

(See **Malt, Tuckers Maltings**.)

The Brewhouse at Haven Reach, Exeter, which is now a big family pub, but used to be a malt-house no doubt serving the likes of Norman & Pring who were just across the river

The Marisco Tavern, Lundy Island, where a two-barrel brewery was set up in 1984

Marisco Tavern Brewery   Lundy Island

This offshore brewery was set up in 1984 on desolate Lundy in the Bristol Channel. A two-barrel brewery was installed in a stable at the Marisco Tavern, the tiny island's only source of alcoholic refreshment, and brewer John Ogilvie set to work. Malt extract was used instead of milled malt, while water came from the island, which could cause problems if rainfall was low. Beers produced were John O's (OG 1035), named after the brewer, Old Light (OG 1040) and Old Light Special (OG 1055); these were named after the Lundy lighthouse which was the highest in the British Isles. Sadly, the brewery closed in 1996 with the disused kit eventually being sold to the Pig on the Hill pub near Bideford, who set up Country Life brewery with it. In 2002, the kit has been on the move again and is now being used for a small brewery in North Somerset, the Tickenham Farm Brewery.

Mash

Process where milled malt is steeped in hot liquor in a mash tun for the purpose of extracting fermentable sugars. This takes several hours and is aided by sparging (or spraying) the mash (as it is known) with hot water to get out all the fermentable sugars. The result is called the sweet wort and tastes rather like Ovaltine. (See **Brewing**.)

Mild

In the 1950s, mild accounted for nearly half of all the beer drunk in the UK. It got its name because of its mild hop rate and low alcoholic volume, though records have shown that the milds of the nineteenth century could be as strong as 7%. At the turn of the last century it was also known as Four Ale. For decades it had been the drink of choice for men working in the thirst-inducing heavy industries of the Midlands, the North and South Wales; as it dropped in strength, mild was a drink of which you could quaff several pints without feeling rough the next morning. Nowadays, like barley wine, it is very much a niche beer, with many breweries only producing milds in May, which CAMRA has long designated Mild Month. Gary Marshall at the Blisland Inn near Bodmin celebrates May with at least 30 milds on tap during the month, including one named after him, King Buddha's Blackbeard Mild (3.2%) from Keltek, who also brew 4X Mild (3.8%). Other brewers in the West Country making mild include Teignworthy and Sutton.

Star Beer: Teignworthy, Martha's Mild (5.3%) – Dark-chestnut brown with flashes of amber, this has a decisive malty nose (breakfast cereal), with a whisper of chocolate from the chocolate malt and a trace of nuttiness; not much hoppiness to be found on the nose. There is a malty start to the palate with a nod in the direction of cocoa powder; mid-palate a spirited citrus (orange peel) fruitiness takes over, lasting the

descent into a dry, bitter-sweet finish, which also has a wisp of chocolate malt making a late surge. More bitter than a mild is supposed to be (mild always has the surname of ale because of its low hopping rate), it is closer to the strength of the original milds of the nineteenth century.

Mildmay Brewery   Holberton, Devon

Brewing started at the Mildmay Colours Inn in late 1993, and the first beers were pulled at Christmas. There were three main beers: Colours Best Bitter (3.8%), Starting Price Ale (4.5%) and 50/1 Porter (5.1%). Production tripled within the first twelve months and other beers were added, including Patrick's Stout (4.2%), George Brendon's Best Bitter (4.5%) and Old Horse Whip (5.7%). Sadly, brewing came to an end in September 1997, though Skinner's of Truro still produce Colours Best and Starting Price for the Mildmay Colours Inn.

Milk Stout

This sweetish stout got its name because it contained milk sugars, or lactose, and was promoted as a beverage with nutritional benefits. Up until 1939, Norman & Pring in Exeter produced a Devonshire Milk Stout, claiming that each pint had 'the energising carbohydrates of 10oz of pure dairy milk'. Milk churns and an image of enduring health also featured strongly on the labels of such beverages, but concerns about drinkers being misled led to MAFF banning the phrase Milk Stout in the late-1940s.

Mill Brewery   Newton Abbot, Devon

Beer enthusiasts Dave Hedge, Paul Bigrig and Simon Swindells set up this brewery in the water treatment plant of a former leather factory in 1983. This was the first brewery in Newton Abbot for many years and they started off with the well-hopped Janners Bitter (OG 1037), which

The Mill Brewery at Newton Abbot

came about after local newspaper readers were asked to name the beer in a competition. Apparently, Janners is the local nickname for a Devonian. Other beers included the malty Janners Old Dark Ale (OG 1040), a strong bitter Janners Old Original (OG 1045) and the Yuletide special Christmas Ale (OG 1050). The brewery was run on a part-time basis until changing hands in 1994. New owners Mike and Liz Cox also started brewing a different guest beer each month, including Whinge Ale (January), Winter Blues (February), St Pat's Tipple (March) and Sam Son (April). Other specials included British Bulldog, which was brewed for the VE celebrations in 1995. However, the beer range was later reduced to concentrate on Janners Ale (3.8%), Old Original (5%) and the winter beer Black Bushel (6%). Mill Brewery closed in 1997.

Mills Brothers   Newton Abbot, Devon

Maltsters, brewers and spirit merchants who operated from Wolborough Road at the end of the nineteenth century until they were bought out by Exeter's St Anne's Well in 1921. John Mills senior was in charge and had a reputation for tyrannical behaviour, which did not go down well with the staff. He had three sons but none of them showed any inclination to join him, and the brewery and its six tied houses went up for sale in 1921, apparently due to the advanced age of Mills senior.

Min Pin Inn   Tregatta near Tintagel, Cornwall
(See **North Cornwall Brewers**.)

One of the late-lamented beers of the Mill Brewery

N *is for*
a noggin of nitro-keg...

Names

In the past brewers were none too bothered about what their regular beers were called and people just asked for mild or bitter. Stronger and more specialist beers such as barley wines and old ales, however, seemed to have a hint of poetry in what they were called, with titles such as Dragon's Blood, Rouser and Colne Spring being common. Brewers also gave some of their beers names which would reflect a regional identity. In the late-1920s, St Austell, or Hicks as they were known then, had a portfolio of draught beers which they imaginatively dubbed XX, XXX, XXXX. In order to compete with the popularity of Bass's bottled ale, they developed a bottled pale ale called Duchy Ale. There was also a Duchy Stout. Names changed in the 1970s and 80s when a new generation of small breweries emerged, many of them having a light-hearted attitude to their beers' names. These days, every brewer wants to make their product instantly memorable. So we have beers with silly names or clever puns on the brewery's name; while others try to reflect their local history or culture or national events like the Queen's Jubilee; then there are the beers which plainly tell the drinker what they are drinking, best bitter, IPA and so on. One of my favourite names is Summerskills Whistle Belly Vengeance. This is a term which apparently comes from the nineteenth century and was the result of drinking too much green, or young, beer!

Nitro-keg

Nitro-keg beers became popular in the mid-1990s, backed by clever advertising campaigns which suggested that many of them had deep Irish or Celtic roots. They had names such as Caffrey's, Wexford and Killkenny, while in the West Country even St Austell joined in with Celtic Smooth and Cornish Cream. Nitro-keg beers were the next generation of keg, brewery-conditioned beers given a clever spin and a large topping of creamy foam, which when settled left the drinker with about 93% of a pint. Short measure indeed. Nitro-keg, just like keg beer, only left the brewery after it had been put through the wringer. First of all it was chilled and the residual yeast filtered out. The beer was now sterile. It was also pasteurised. Keg beer was pumped full of carbon dioxide to make it resemble live beer, but in reality it came across as a cold, bland and very fizzy product. Nitro-keg went for a mixture of gases dominated by nitrogen, which made the beer less gassy, but no less cold and bland. Smoothflow beers are of the same family.

Norman & Pring   Exeter, Devon

Brewing is supposed to have started in the late-seventeenth century at the City Brewery site adjacent to the ancient Exe Bridge, on a spot named Exe Island, when Robert Vilvaine wished to raise money to send scholarship boys to Oxford. Brewing was his way of financing this wish. In the eighteenth and nineteenth centuries, there was a variety of brewing partnerships, under which the business grew until JE Norman brought in Walter Pring as a business partner. Norman & Pring went on to become the biggest brewers in Exeter, if not in Devon. A price-list from 1940 sees mild at £7.50 a cask, BB (best bitter) and stout £8.60 a cask and XXX Burton £9.40. The Second World War also saw Norman & Pring partially merging with competitors St Anne's

Above: *Norman & Pring's City Brewery*
Below: *Workers at Norman & Pring in the early years of the twentieth century*

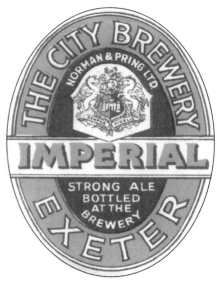

Above left: *Steam-driven delivery vehicles from Norman & Pring*
Left: *Norman & Pring Leyland Beaver delivery lorry at the brewery in 1957*

Trade exhibition at Norman & Pring's
City Brewery, 1955, note ads for Pale Ale
and Scotch Ale

Well, though a complete merger took place in the mid-1950s with the latter going into voluntary liquidation in 1960. Brewing was transferred to the St Anne's site, while the City Brewery was used for bottling. In 1955 Norman & Pring put themselves under the Whitbread 'umbrella', as did many regional breweries of the time. This was supposed to be good for them, but a takeover followed in 1962 with well over 150 tied houses being consumed. At the time, Norman & Pring said that the reason for the deal was that they faced the herculean task of building a new brewery, as their own was threatened by a local development scheme. One of the directors seemed to know that the end was near though, as he was quoted as saying that there had been four generations of Prings in the brewery. He seemed to be hinting that there would not be a fifth. Soon afterwards the business was amalgamated with Starkey, Knight & Ford, and bottling was transferred to Tiverton. The City Brewery site went up for sale, and the name of Norman & Pring vanished for good from the Exeter scene. As if to truly finalise the end, a fire destroyed the brewery in the late-1960s and the site was redeveloped when the old bridge was replaced. Beers lost for good included Nap Pale Ale, Imperial Strong Ale, Oatmeal Stout and Double Brown Ale.

North Cornwall Brewers   Min Pin Inn, Tregatta near Tintagel, Cornwall

Girl-power was the distinctive added ingredient when this brew-pub was opened in an old farmhouse in May 1986 by the only all-female brewing team in the country, Marie Hall and her daughter Stephanie. It was a small operation using malt extract, with two beers being produced, Legend Bitter (OG 1036) and the full-bodied Brown Willy (OG 1055). The pub's name came from the miniature Pinscher dogs bred by the owners. Brewing stopped in 1994.

Above: *Min Pin Inn, home of the North Cornwall Brewers*
Right: *North Cornwall Brewers' barrels at the Min Pin Inn*

O *is for*
organic, otters and others...

Octagon Brewery   Plymouth, Devon

Set up in 1861 by Joseph Godfrey, this brewery was based in Martin Street and owned 48 pubs. One of its more popular beers was OB Stout which was described on the label as 'nourishing and digestive'. The company lost its independence in 1954 when Simonds bought everything up (incidentally, this was the same year as an unexploded German bomb was found near the brewery), but brewing at the site continued until 1970.

O'Hanlon's   Whimple, Devon

Though many people make that move from town to country, few, if any, take their own brewery with them. But that is exactly what John and Liz O'Hanlon and their two children did when they moved from London to deepest Devon in 2000. Not only did the kit travel down the M5, but head brewer Alex Bell and assistant Richard Mayne came too. Until then, O'Hanlon's was based beneath a railway arch in South London, and it was also the name of an excellent pub run by John in Clerkenwell, which served as the brewery tap. However, it was all becoming too much and the brewery needed more space,

O'Hanlon's Brewery (left), and the owners' seventeenth-century farmhouse

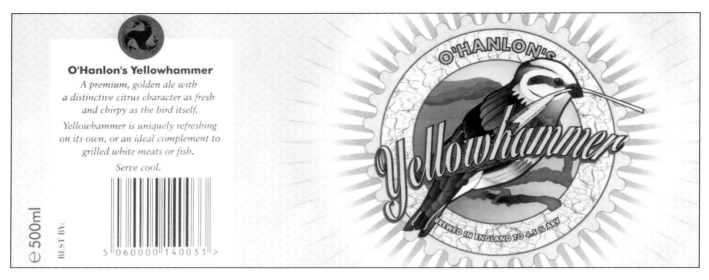

Top: *O'Hanlon's Yellowhammer*
Above: *At O'Hanlon's Brewery, with John O'Hanlon (left) and brewer Alex Bell*

which they found in the form of a seventeenth-century farmhouse, several barns and 25 acres near the village of Whimple, in undulating countryside south of Exeter. The place seemed ideal but Liz and John had to do extensive research before acting. The water supply was checked – they have their own well – and a diviner called in to locate a secondary source of water. The O'Hanlons finally moved in during the summer of 2000 and started brewing in November.

Now, their eight-barrel brewery, which has been with them since they began in 1996, is located in a roomy barn. There is plenty of room for their gleaming fermenting vessels, and there are pallets of bottled beers stacked around ready to be delivered. O'Hanlon's also brew and bottle beer for other micro-brewers. On the beer side of things, John says, 'We've tried to be as innovative as possible while hanging on to the core beers.' Hops used include Challenger, Phoenix, Cascade, Saaz and Styrian Goldings as well as organic Hallertau. Other ingredients used are bog myrtle, honey and port. 'We like our beers to have intriguing flavours,' says Liz.

Even though O'Hanlon's are noted for their eclectic ales, the bricks and mortar of their portfolio are the light session ale Firefly, Blakeley's Best, a best bitter with a Cascade hop citrusy character, and Red Ale. Alongside these you will find the likes of the spicy and dry Myrica Ale, which uses bog myrtle instead of hops, with honey balancing the bitterness of the herb, and the summer ale Yellowhammer. However, it is the bottle-conditioned beers which have really made a name for O'Hanlon's: the award-winning Wheat Beer, the scrumptious Organic Rye Beer and a delicious Port Stout, which won a silver medal at the 2002 Beer World Cup in the States. John says:

Our original dry stout worked well for us, but I wanted to add port to a stout – it is an old Irish hangover cure! I spoke to a wine merchant and he suggested Ferrera Port which is the biggest brand in Portugal. We put half a bottle in each cask.

O'Hanlon's is country brewing at its best. Dogs, horses, a miniature pony and a pot-bellied pig give the homestead an idyllic rural air. The thatched farmhouse has cob walls and the living room boasts an amazing fireplace with nooks and crannies for baking bread. A local farming neighbour gets the spent malt for his beef cattle, and he in turn loans the O'Hanlons a tractor when needed. 'All good proper country stuff,' says John. It is a far cry from south London. (See **Red Ale, Rye, Stout**.)

Beers: Firefly (3.7%); Wheat Beer (4%); Blakeley's Best (4.2%); Myrica Ale (4.2%); Dry Stout (4.2%); Original Port Stout (4.4%); Red Ale (4.5%). Occasional: Yellowhammer (4.5%). Bottles: Wheat Beer; Original Port Stout (4.8%); Organic Rye Beer (5%), bottle-conditioned. Myrica Ale has also been bottle-conditioned under the name of Bog Myrtle.

Star Beer: Wheat Beer (4%) – This wonderful wheat beer looks to the Anglo-American wheaten beer style rather than the bananas and cloves of Munich Weissens. Yellow-gold in colour, there is a delicate citrusy aroma on the nose. On the palate first impressions are of a soft, rounded maltiness leading to a refreshing tangy and hoppy finish. As the beer develops there are hints of more hops on the nose, and a slight effervescense is noticeable on the tongue along with an emerging fruitiness.

Recommended pubs: Blacksmith's Arms, Plymtree; Well House, Exeter.

Old Ale

The dark, warming beers produced for the winter months are known variously as old ales, winter ales and Christmas ales; not to be confused with barley wines, which are equally strong and seasonal. Old ales

usually have bags of fruit, rich malt and good hoppiness on the nose, while the palate is complex, malty, sometimes slightly sweet, and always finished with a generous amount of hoppiness to stop over-cloying. Because of drink-driving laws and a general change in drinking habits, old ales are not as common as they used to be though many Westcountry brewers make at least one brew of them. Ones to look for include Beer Engine's Whistlemass (strength varies), and Teignworthy's Christmas Cracker (6%). (See **Winter Ales**.)

Old Ferry Brewery   Saltash, Cornwall

Brewery which was due to open in 1984 but never really got under steam. Three beers were promised: Tuffy's Ale (OG 1039), Bosun's Bitter (OG 1045) and Admiral's 'Ard (OG 1060).

Organic Beer

The organic beer sector has been growing in leaps and bounds in the last few years, with several Westcountry brewers producing Soil Association approved beers. In Cornwall, there is even a totally organic brewery. What is the lure of organic beer? Part of it seems to be the fact that more of us want the best ingredients these days, and there is no doubt that we feel that we are getting the best when we buy organic. We also want to be more environmentally friendly, and organic materials are free of pesticides and genetic modifications. According to Andy Hamer at the Organic Brewhouse:

Non-organic hops are sprayed 16 times in season, but with organic ones, they grow clover in between the rows, and that attracts the predators who would usually go for the aphids on the hops. Non-organic barley is also sprayed as a matter of course.

Not everyone is convinced by organic beer. St Austell's head brewer Roger Ryman does not envisage them producing an organic beer:

With organic raw materials the primary selection of ingredients is that they are organic. I am concerned at the quality of organic ingredients, it seems that you have to take what you can get. I brew the best quality beers that I can from non-organic materials; I use 100 per cent malt, whole leaf hops, and no chemicals. I don't want to sacrifice this quality for beers whose ingredients are going to be inconsistent just for the sake of calling them organic.

After all the pros and cons, what does organic beer taste like? Are we being presented with wonderful examples which will knock spots off ordinary non-organic ones? Most brewers would agree that it is the recipe of the beer, which will win over the palate, organic or non-organic. It is no good going to all the trouble to produce a natural ale if it tastes horrible. According to Liz O'Hanlon at O'Hanlon's, who produce an organic rye beer:

I think organic beers are a lifestyle choice. They don't always necessarily taste any better, but people want them because they know the ingredients are free from pesticides.

Andy Hamer takes a slightly different view:

Organic beers seem to taste better than non-organic ones. There seems to be a cleanness of flavour, and people who have drunk the bottled versions of my beers say that they have a fuller flavour.

And that is what good beer, organic or not, is all about – flavour.

Organic Brewhouse   Cury Cross Lanes, Cornwall

Andy Hamer is Bolton born-and-bred, with the accent to match, but these days he regards his home as Cornwall, where he set up his all-organic brewery in April 2000, one of the first in the UK. A few months prior to that he had already been down to Cornwall with a brewery in mind and even found a possible site. So when his boss back up North said he was looking for voluntary redundancies, the keen home-brewer leapt at the chance. As the plans for his enterprise whirled around his head, he would often go down to the Bank Top Brewery in Bolton and ask questions, help out with the mash tun and learn about making beer on a bigger scale than he was used to.

Why organic? 'Just for the sake of the planet, but I'm no health freak,' he says as he lights up a roll-up. It has not been plain sailing going

Organic Brewhouse's Andy Hamer carries out 'quality control'

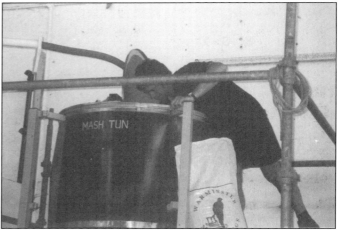

Above: *Inside the roomy confines of the Organic Brewhouse*
Above right: *Andy Hamer checks out his mash tun*

organic. Initially he could only get one variety of hop, Hallertau, which is an aroma hop with a light, flowery character. 'The idea of being only able to get one variety of hop worried me at first,' he says, 'but I think it is a good thing at the end of the day.' However, he hopes to be getting three more varieties of organic hop later in the year, including the classic English hop Goldings, so the character of the beers should become more hoppy. At the moment they are pretty malty and dry. As for organic malt, there was more variety on the market with pale malt, chocolate, wheat and crystal all being readily available.

THE ORGANIC BREWHOUSE

WOLF ROCK

CASK CONDITIONED ORGANIC ALE

5.0% A.B.V.

SOIL ASSOCIATION ORGANIC STANDARD

ORGANIC CERTIFICATION, U.K.5

Brewed on the Lizard Peninsula, Cornwall, using organically grown barley, wheat and hops.

The Organic Brewhouse is a seven-barrel plant, based in a roomy space on a small rural workshop site, off the road from Helston to Land's End. In fact the kit looks rather lost in its home, which apparently used to be an abattoir. Andy lives right next door. Sampling his beers outside in the sun with a view of distant fields, there is nothing to disturb the silence, until a visit from what Andy calls his quality controllers – local lads from the site or nearby who often drop by for a pint.

As for the beers, there are four regulars, Lizard Point, Serpentine, Black Rock Stout and Wolf Rock, all called after local points of geological interest. Serpentine, for instance, is named after the rock formation which stretches beneath the Lizard peninsula; a very old and hard rock which was used for building lighthouses. As for the future, Andy has plans to produce a few speciality beers. 'I've often fancied bay leaves as a flavour,' he says. A pub would also be a good investment, which undoubtedly would major on good beer and music, as Andy is also a bass musician. He says:

I play in a rock-and-pop covers band called Best Served Chilled. I've played in bands for donkey's years. Out here I do one gig a week. It keeps the wolf from the door.

Or the Wolf Rock in his case.

Beers: Lizard Point (4%); Serpentine (4.5%); Black Rock Stout (4.7%); Wolf Rock (5%). Bottles: Serpentine; Black Rock Stout; both bottle-conditioned.

Star Beer: Black Rock Stout (4.7%) – Very dark in colour with brown tints; there is a heady, comforting nose of chocolate and mocha coffee, while the palate has smoky, coffee-bean and chocolate-flavour notes, with a background of citrus fruit (lemon/lime). The finish is bitter, fruity and dry which lingers, making you ready for another slurp. An intensely satisfying stout style.

Recommended outlets: Halzephron Inn, Gunwalloe; Star & Garter, Falmouth.

Original Gravity

Unit of measurement of the strength of a beer, based on the amount of dissolved fermentable malt sugars present in the wort after the mash has taken place. Water is defined as having an original gravity of 1000, so a beer with an original gravity of 1040 (the usual amount for ordinary bitter) is approximately 4% denser than the water. A higher original gravity means that a stronger beer will be brewed, though the measurement will decline after fermentation because of the yeast's action on malt sugars. Original gravity was used by the Customs & Excise to work out how much duty should be paid. Until a few years ago beers declared their strength by stating their original gravity on handpumps and bottle labels, but it has now changed to alcohol by volume, which is measured after the beer has been fermented. (See **ABV**.)

Otter Brewery   Luppitt, Devon

At the end of the 1980s, David McCaig was working for Whitbread at their Liverpool plant. A closure was on the cards and McCaig was offered a job brewing in Malawi. The alternative was retirement. He took the latter option and came to Fordwater, near Axminster, where he started making furniture. But once a brewer, always a brewer. In 1990 he set up Otter Brewery at an old farm high up in the hills north of Honiton. As the headspring of the Otter River was very close there really could be only one name for the enterprise. Patrick McCaig, who joined his father's brewery fulltime in 1995, says:

We started with three beers, Bitter, Ale and Head. David had worked with Whitbread, had seen how beer was brewed and realised that on a smaller

Above: *The view from Otter Brewery*
Right: *Otter Brewery, where 100 barrels of beer are brewed each week*

Otter's Patrick McCaig in the brewery

scale he could craft his with more care and finesse. It started off as a five-barrel plant and things went exceptionally well.

Now they are a 30-barrel plant, brewing on average 100 barrels a week throughout the whole year, while their beers can be found at over 130 outlets throughout Somerset, Dorset and Devon, including the Heavitree pub estate, which is rarely open to smaller brewers. The brewery (and family home) is in a beautiful location hidden down a winding track, where an old farm complex has been converted. Tree-covered hills and wooded combes surround the spot. It is an ideal hideaway, but near enough to the A303 for swift transportation of the beer into the bars of the West Country and beyond. Water comes from a spring on the brewery's land, while the hops are mainly Challenger

Pub Life No.1

"It was this big!"

Relax with an Otter

The Otter Brewery

and Fuggles, which Otter use to produce muscular beers with a great tang factor and an almost northern bitterness in some.

There are four main beers, the three with which David McCaig began, plus Otter Bright. The bitter is a flavoursome session beer with a grainy, toasty malty character on the palate, leading to a dry and bitter hoppy finish. Ale is a gum-tinglingly hoppy bitter with a good malty, grainy balance, and a lasting bitter finish. Bright is a refreshing golden beer which can be served cooler than the other ales. The final beer in the Otter quartet is the excellent Otter Head. Patrick adds:

We also have a beer which starts off as Witch Otter. Then it becomes Otter Claus for Christmas, MacOtter for Burns Night and finally Cupid's Otter for St Valentine's Day. It is the same beer with a different name all the year round.

As well as their beers, Otter are known for their light-hearted posters and beer-mats. Given his background in advertising and marketing, Patrick must have realised long ago that the brewery needed more than brilliant beer to reach out to people who do not always choose real ale. Hence the birth of the brewery's own otter, a highly stylised beast which is more Picasso than Tarka, and who turns up on the brewery's publicity items. Patrick explains the origins of this characterful, beer-drinking mammal:

When we developed it we could have done a cute pretty one but we had a younger, more versatile image done. The result of a boardroom brain-storming session? *No, we came up with the image one drunken night.*

…Or well-ottered, as the posters say.

Beers: Bitter (3.6%); Bright (4.3%); Ale (4.5%); Head (5.8%). Occasional: Claus (5%). Bottles: Bitter; Bright; Ale; Claus; Head.

Star Beer: Otter Head (5.8%) – A big-tasting, flavoursome strong ale with toffee, rich malt and resiny hop aromas on the nose. On the palate there is rich malt, fruitiness, nuttiness, vinous fruit and even a trace of chocolate, which is balanced by a resiny hoppy finish with a lasting dryness. A wonderful beer.

Recommended outlets: Turf Locks, Exminster; Drewe Arms, Broadhembury.

P *is for*
pub and a pint of porter...

Pale Ale

Beer style that emerged from IPAs when drinkers began to demand weaker beers. At the same time, draught bitter became popular and pale ales were seen as their bottled counterparts. The colour of draught bitter ranged from pale to dark, while pale ales were not as pale as the name would suggest and certainly not as bitter as IPAs. A touch of crystal malt gave pale ale a bronze or amber tint and also produced a nutty, malty roundedness which was balanced by hops and a delicious fruitiness. During the keg years, pale ale became a bit of a dirty word among beer connoisseurs who took it to mean weak, gassy bottled beers lingering for ages in the recesses of a pub. In the West Country, examples of the style included Norman & Pring's City Pale Ale and St Austell's Duchy Special Pale Ale, which apparently had a good hop flavour. Nowadays, few if any Westcountry brewers call their beers pale ales, though echoes of the style linger on in best bitters. (**See Bitter, IPA.**)

Pasteurisation

Once beer is brewed it can be left to continue its secondary fermentation or it can be filtered and pasteurised before being bottled, canned or kegged. Named after Louis Pasteur, pasteurisation involves treating filtered beer with heat for the purpose of killing off any remaining yeast cells. This leaves the beer dead and sterile and can also give it a cooked flavour. On the other hand, pasteurisation has its champions, such as Peter Hawksley at the Beer Engine, whose bottled Piston Bitter is pasteurised. 'That way you can get a decent shelf life,' he says. 'Bottle-conditioning mystifies the public with all the yeast floating about in the bottom.'

Pensans Brews   Gulval, near Penzance, Cornwall

At the start of 1983, Blue Anchor brewer Tim Sears also set up this brewery in a small village in the extreme south-west of Cornwall. A local farmer provided an old milking shed and the kit was home-made. First beer out of the racks was Coref Pensans (OG 1045), Cornish for

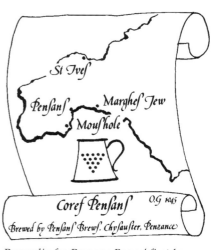

Pumpclip for Pensans Brews' first beer

Penzance Ale. Other beers included Coref Ertach Pensans (OG 1055), specially brewed to celebrate Penzance's heritage fortnight in May, and MSB (OG 1055), otherwise known as Mak's Special Beer. Sadly, Tim Sears could not find sufficient regular trade in an area dependent on holiday-makers, and the operation shut down in the summer of 1985. (See **Blue Anchor**.)

E Petter & Son   Barnstaple, Devon

Edwin Petter started off as a maltster and dealer in Peruvian guano before starting to brew in 1881 at the newly built Anchor Brewery. Beer-making did not last long when the company and his ten pubs were swallowed up by Hancock's. There is no record of what happened to the business of bird-droppings...

Pinsent & Sons   Newton Abbot, Devon

Not content with brewing, Pinsent were also maltsters, wine and spirit merchants. They even shifted coal. Set up in the second half of the nineteenth century, the brewery had a tied estate of 38 houses, including pubs which are still familiar to Newton Abbot's locals today – the Market House Inn and the Courtenay Arms. William Swain Pinsent, the son of the original founder, retired at the end of the First World War, and the brewery was sold to Heavitree of Exeter. Brewing stopped on the site, although the new owners used it as a bottling depot and branch office.

Plymouth Breweries   Plymouth, Devon

In 1889 four city breweries and one from Saltash just over the Tamar got together to form Plymouth Breweries. The brewery was based at the

The Plymouth Brewery, home of Heavy, a cross between a mild and a porter according to Carl Beeson of Summerskills Brewery

Regent Brewery in Stonehouse in Plymouth, and carried on until 1970 when it was bought by the Courage group for £6.5 million. Right up until the end it was gloriously old-fashioned with wooden barrels and horse-drawn drays. Brewing carried on under the banner of Courage (Plymouth), with a Best Bitter (OG 1039) and Heavy (OG 1032), which despite its name was actually a mild. Sadly, fans of Heavy were not happy with Courage's attempts at brewing it, as Carl Beeson of Summerskills remembers, 'I used to drink Heavy before it was buggered up by Courage. It was a beautiful beer, a cross between a mild and a porter.' Another Plymouth drinker recalled, 'The Heavy didn't have a very good name. It was renowned to have everything in it they couldn't use.' Brewing stopped in 1983 and the brewery's site is now home to a motor-cruiser builders.

Points West   Plymouth, Devon

Students are known for enjoying a drop or two and those who attend the Plymouth College of Further Education are luckier than most. As well as the usual student union bar, this college has its own brewery, a five-barrel unit which can be seen through a glass wall from the campus coffee shop. Overseen by former policeman, long-time home-brewer and stalwart CAMRA member Roger Pengelly, Points West came into being a couple of years back with the aim of giving those students who needed it, experience of the licensing trade. Apparently the EU also put up some money, stipulating that the brewery only use local or English raw materials. This means that Roger is very dependent on Goldings and Fuggles hops, which is no bad thing. The European connection does not end there. Roger, who also teaches at the college, occasionally gets to spend a week in Belgium and Munich studying traditional beers – all in the name of research of course.

Points West's Drake's Drum celebrates one of Devon's favourite sons, and appropriately enough can be found at Drake's former home

Points West started out with two beers, HLB (4%) and a dark beer called Black Out (4.6%). These are long gone and the brewery's main beers are currently Pilgrim, which is described as a light-coloured bitter with a sweetish finish because that is what the students like, and Drake's Drum. This dangerously drinkable golden beer is brewed especially for the National Trust where it can be found in bottle-conditioned form at a couple of Westcountry National Trust houses, including Buckland Abbey, north of Plymouth. It is also available on draught, where it goes down well at the bar of lucky old Plymouth Argyle. Also brewed for the National

Trust is Medieval Ale, a liquoricy stout with roast barley in the grist. There is also their Winter Ale, which Roger describes as a Trappist Ale style.

However, Points West's beers are not easy to find, as Roger Pengelly explains:

> Because we are not a business, other Devon brewers didn't think it was fair that we were sending our beers into the trade, so now pubs have to approach us and licensees are not noted for picking up the phone.

But he does say that the Boringdon Arms in Turnchapel, Plymouth, and the Blisland Inn, near Bodmin, have been known to take a cask or two of Pilgrim (where it is sold as Pilgrim PA), and local beer festivals also feature Roger's beers. So the intrepid beer hunter, if he or she wants to add Points West's beers to their list, should either call the pubs mentioned, develop a sudden interest in country houses, start going to see how Plymouth get on in the Second Division, or enrol at the college. Failing that, persuade your landlord to pick up the phone!

Beers: Pilgrim (4.2%); Drake's Drum (4.8%); Winter Ale (7.5%). Bottles: Drake's Drum; Medieval Ale (4.4%), both bottle-conditioned; available from Buckland Abbey.

Star Beer: Drake's Drum (4.8%) – Very pale in colour; fruity (fruit jelly), citrusy nose with a hint of grainy maltiness. Initial grainy malt is supplanted by citrus fruit and peppery hop, leading to a long, gentle bitter finish, which has some fruitiness in it. Delicious.

Cotleigh Brewery's enduring interest in birds of prey continues with Peregrine Porter

Porter

Full-flavoured, fruity and hoppy dark beer believed to have first appeared in the 1720s in east London when Ralph Harwood brewed something called Entire. This was a style of beer which was very popular in London but not so with landlords who had to blend three styles, or 'threads', in their cellar. Harwood's venture, which was to be called porter, saved them the work. No one really knows how porter got its name, but one theory suggests it came from its popularity with the market porters working in the East End. Whatever the story, porter hit gold in the eighteenth century and brewers across the land went into overdrive to satisfy the thirst for this strong, dark beverage. However, the following century saw porter become indelibly associated with the working classes, as their so-

Porter tuns maturing at Norman & Pring, probably some time before the First World War when fuel restrictions put paid to porter

called superiors turned to IPAs and then pale ales. Offshoots of porter included stout and imperial porters or stouts.

The story of porter after this was one of a slow and then sudden decline, not helped by the First World War when the British Government put a ban on dark, highly roasted or kilned malts in order to conserve fuel. This ban did not apply in Ireland for political reasons and Guinness had a clear run on the market. Whitbread, one of the great porter breweries, rolled out its last barrel during the war. Throughout the 1950s and 60s the nearest most drinkers got to a pint of porter was seeing the word engraved on the windows or sculptured on the stonework of pubs. As for Guinness, it brewed its last porter in 1974. Porter was dead. Or was it? During the last couple of decades the sleeping giant of porter has been revived by dozens of small breweries dedicated to preserving some of our brewing history. Notable Westcountry examples of porter come from the Beer Engine, Sutton, Cotleigh, Exmoor and Scattor Rock. Long may it continue.

Star Beer: Exmoor Ales Beast (6.6%) – A very strong porter, dark in colour with reddish-brown highlights. On the nose there is espresso coffee, dried fruit (currants, raisins), even the merest hint of brandy or rum. The palate is satisfyingly complex and smooth with fruit cake, coffee bean and dark malt, balanced by a good hoppiness, leading to a lasting and bitter finish.

Princetown Brewery

Princetown's Simon Loveless is a brewer by trade. He started off with Wiltshire family brewers Gibbs Mew and then went on to Salisbury-based Hop Back. Wanting to brew his own beer, he went in search of a business partner, hoping to find either a small beer wholesaling company or a modest pub group wishing to add brewing to their operations. As luck would have it, he met a hotel owner looking to expand into the South West who had come across the Prince of Wales pub in Princetown, which was for sale. The semi-derelict buildings at the back of the pub were ideal for a brewery. The two men did a deal and the first pint from Princetown Brewery was pulled in late 1994, after the run-down granite building, originally home to an old boat, was rebuilt.

It started as a four-barrel plant, brewing twice a week. Nowadays the capacity for one brew is 15 barrels and during busy summer months Simon is brewing three times a week. Along with Simon, who is also managing director, the brewery employs an assistant and a driver. To many, Princetown can seem a bleak and remote place, especially in

The Prince of Wales in Princetown, where Simon Loveless' beers can be sampled

winter, and the last place you would expect to find a thriving independent brewery, though Simon once delved back into local records, discovering that 'in the early days when they first built the prison, the officers' mess had a brewery which operated for about twelve months'. However, Simon's beers have become firm favourites with local real ale drinkers and have won many awards at beer festivals, both local and national. Even the Royal Family, who have never been noted beer drinkers, have got in on the act. A couple of years after the brewery went on stream, the Prince of Wales, performed its official opening. Simon sent Charles off with a case or two of a specially brewed beer, HRH Ale.

Above left: *By royal appointment: Princetown Brewery*
Above: *Simon Loveless at Princetown Brewery*

There are two Princetown beers – Dartmoor IPA and Jail Ale; while there used to be a 5% Dartmoor Gold. 'You can produce a more consistent product if you limit the beers brewed,' says Simon. 'It is about building up a brand. If we were producing a dozen different beers with obscure names then I feel that the brand identity would be lost.' As for ingredients, they are all local – Simon is a great believer in keeping things as neighbourly as possible, explaining:

All the hops are English, Challenger for bitterness and Goldings for aroma hopping, while it is the brewery's own yeast strain which is slightly fruity. The water is mains water from Dartmoor, which is very good. With both beers I'm looking for a moreishness so that if you have had a pint then you want another one.

Like many Westcountry breweries, Princetown is a great example of keeping brewing in the community. It seems ludicrous to Simon Loveless that Devonian beer has to travel 'up country' to be sold. 'Keep local beers local,' seems to be his slogan and those drinkers who frequent the pubs of Dartmoor and drink his ales would certainly raise a glass to that.

Beers: Dartmoor IPA (4%); Jail Ale (4.8%). Bottles: Jail Ale, bottle-conditioned.

Star Beer: Princetown IPA (4%) – Amber-coloured best bitter with a hoppy and fruity (apricot) nose. On the palate, biscuit malt kicks off the show before a fruity mid-palate, which leads to a lasting bitter finish while retaining some of the mid-palate fruitiness. A thirst-quenching, well-balanced beer.

Recommended pubs: Prince of Wales, Princetown; Plume of Feathers, Princetown.

Pub

One of Britain's greatest achievements, the pub is a licensed house where people can gather, talk, play games such as the old Westcountry favourite skittles and, of course, drink good beer. The Romans got in on the act first by providing lodgings at regular intervals on their roads where travellers could rest and recuperate (the original 'taverna' which gave rise to the word tavern). Centuries later, it was the turn of the monasteries to offer sustenance and home-brewed beer. These were the first inns. In the towns taverns and alehouses developed, the latter being private houses where local people enjoyed their pints. It was not until the nineteenth century that the public house assumed its dominant role in British society. As brewers grew larger and bought up establishments through which to sell their beers, public houses became more decorative and ornate. Segregated areas also developed: the snug, the public bar, the lounge, the parlour, the smoke room and the jug and bottle (this being the place you would visit if you wanted to take some beer home with you).

Some of these Victorian pubs were incredibly grandiose and lavish, with engraved plate-glass windows and mirrors, mahogany wood and polished brass fittings, and moulded plaster ceilings. Temperance movements inevitably tried to paint a much darker picture. But while there have always been (and always will be) dingy dives with a suspect clientele and dreadful beer, the pub at its best is a community centre which just happens to sell beer. You can sit and read your paper, have something to eat, catch up on local gossip or just mull over the day with your pint. The last few decades has seen the pub under pressure as rural ones close at the rate of knots, while town and city ones are gutted to fit in with whatever trend their brewery or pub company owner thinks is fashionable. Luckily the West Country is blessed with a high proportion of good, honest pubs many of which are free houses, which means that they offer a good selection of real ales. To experience a truly unspoilt pub visit the Dolphin in the Barbican in Plymouth, which, although owned by a pub company, has remained untouched. The windows are the original ones put in by the Octagon Brewery, who owned the place until the 1950s.

Pub Group

A company which owns pubs but does not brew beer. Some of the groups, such as Punch Taverns, holds thousands of pubs, others have just a few. Some beer-drinkers complain that pub groups limit choice, with landlords' option of guest ales confined to the usual big brewery suspects.

Pub Names

The history of pub names in this country needs (and has had) a whole book to itself. Throughout the centuries, the names provide a reflection of this country's history and its people. Pubs have been named after historical events, famous people, royal symbols, various trades, animals, local pastimes, local monuments and saints. For instance, the

The sign and the name of the Beer Engine at Newton St Cyres reflects the pub's past history in dealing with a once thriving railway-based trade

Rising Sun comes from the badge of Edward III, which depicted the sun in splendour; the Blue Peter Inn (you will find one in Polperro) comes from the naval flag, while the Drewe Arms in Broadhembury is named after the Drewe family who owned the nearby Castle Drogo. The Powder Monkey in Torquay is called after a local woman who ended up in the Navy as a powder monkey, filling shells and bullets with powder. The splendid tradition of pub names has been threatened in the last few years with the emergence of joky names such as The Ferret and Drainpipe or Cucumber and Lettuce. They mean nothing apart from the passing fads of advertising folk, and will keep changing to conform with the whims of customers – but there will always be a Royal Oak or a Fox and Hounds – won't there?

Pumpclip

Colourful card attached to the front of a handpump, giving the name of the beer and brewery plus an image of what the brewery wants to convey. Some pumpclips are whacky, irreverent and almost cartoonish, while others go for the heritage look. Pumpclips are collectable, though no one has devised a name for the collector.

R *is for*
real ale and a really thirsty pig!...

Real Ale

Before the onset of kegged beers in the 1960s, all beer was real, undergoing a secondary fermentation in the cask. The term real ale was coined in the 1970s by the founders of CAMRA as they campaigned against the fizzy, dead beers which were gradually supplanting traditional beers. Nowadays, we take it to mean beer, made from natural ingredients, which matures in the cask (or bottle) and does not have extraneous carbon dioxide. It is also called cask-conditioned ale. (See **CAMRA**.)

Red Ale

According to John O'Hanlon who produces a marvellous Red Ale, this was an old Irish style of beer. He takes up the story:

The Irish, like the Scots, didn't have the climate for growing hops and so they would have sweetish tasting beers which would have been seasoned with herbs and spices. A lot of the malt kilned over the peat would have given that colour to the grain.

Star Beer: O'Hanlon's Red Ale (5%) – A very dry beer, the colour of a copper pan; on the nose there are bags of dried fruit; plenty of malt and fruitiness, including baked banana, on the palate, before a lasting bitter-sweet and dry finish. Complex, full of flavour and thirst-quenching.

Redruth Brewery   Redruth, Cornwall

There has been a brewery in Redruth since 1742 when William Davey started brewing beer for the thousands of miners who had flocked to the town for work in the local copper mines. It became the Redruth Brewery Company in the nineteenth century, and remained with this name until JA Devenish bought them in the 1930s. The Redruth end of the Devenish operation became a considerably larger concern with up to 200 people being employed on the site at the height of its success. Change came in the 1980s when Devenish fell victim to a takeover and

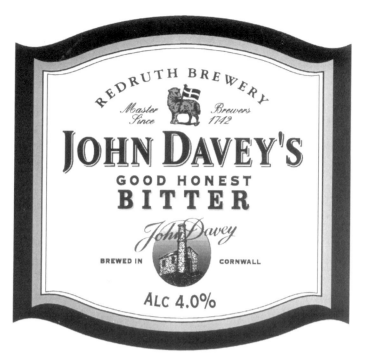

Redruth Brewery's John Davey's Bitter which recalls the man who started brewing in Redruth in 1742

the brewing side of things underwent a management buyout, with the current Redruth Brewery re-emerging to join the brewing fray once again. Currently owned by a Hong-Kong-based brewery, Redruth is not a big manufacturer of cask-conditioned ales. 'A greater proportion of our beers go into the take-home market in the shape of bottles and cans,' says head brewer George Roe, who used to work for the now defunct Mansfield Brewery. 'Our volumes of cask-conditioned ale aren't enormous and we don't brew it all the year round.'

The brewery keeps its cards close to its chest as well. The brew-length, for instance, is 'confidential'. Redruth currently brews three cask-conditioned ales, and there have also been seasonal beers in recent years, including Rudolph the Redruth Brain Beer (5.5%). These are traditional tasting beers with plenty of malt character and a good balance of hops. As for finding them in the pubs in Cornwall, this is definitely a job for the dedicated beer-hunter, as most of the cask-conditioned beer is distributed by wholesalers throughout the whole country. This seems a shame, as Redruth Brewery has a valuable inheritance as custodian of a great Cornish brewing tradition. (See **JA Devenish**.)

Beers: Cornish Original (4.1%); Cornish Rebellion (4.8%); Cornish Steam Brewed Bitter (5%). Bottles: John Davey's Bitter (4.5%); Cornish Rebellion; Redruth Steam Beer (5%); Redruth Steam Lager (5%).

Star Beer: Cornish Original (4.1%) – Chestnut-brown colour. On the polished nose there is a nutty maltiness which is very reminiscent of Wadworth's 6X. A gentle breeze of fruitiness and resiny hop is also noticeable. On the palate, there is more malty nuttiness plus hints of toffee, followed by a mid-palate fruitiness leading to a hoppy and dry finish. Based on the old Devenish recipe.

Ring O' Bells   Launceston, Cornwall

Heard the one about the pig who drank beer? When Adrian Carter set up the Ring O' Bells brewery in the village of North Hill in 1999, his chief taster was the family pet, a house-trained Vietnamese pot-bellied porker called Monty. He recalls:

Adrian Carter at the Ring O' Bells Brewery

When we were brewing in the pub, I had a couple of beers up on stillage, so that people who visited the brewery could have a drink. The barrels kept being emptied and I thought it was the local kids. But once when I was in the garden Monty came out of the house and made his way towards where the beers were stored. He opened the door to the cellar with his snout, and I crept over to look in the window. He was turning the tap to the beer and letting it fill the bucket underneath and then drinking it.

Owner (and occasional brewer) Adrian Carter is a blunt-speaking Yorkshireman who had been a home-brewer all his life. He also had a go at making whisky when he was a schoolboy. This ended up with him being expelled from school chemistry lessons for distilling in the labs. As well as being in the Army, he has managed pubs and worked for a major brewery in the North of England. But it was not until he came down to Cornwall in the late-1990s that he started to think seriously about brewing and bought the Ring O' Bells pub in North Hill, near Launceston. This was a medieval ciderhouse and more latterly an alehouse which had closed in 1918 after the death of a local when he was thrown from a cart. Adrian says:

I found a cider-press which dated back to the Middle Ages, and I thought it would be nice to turn part of the building back to an old brewery. Problem was that every time I made my own home-brew it kept going off due to the wild yeast in the walls of the old alehouse. Samples of it were sent to a lab, and they found the place humming with yeast.

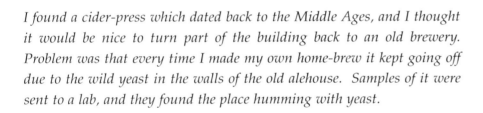

One of the Ring O' Bells beers which commemorates Monty the Vietnamese pot-bellied pig

The upshot of all this was that, with the help of two microbiologists, the old yeast strain was reincubated and is now used to ferment today's beers. After running into planning problems Adrian decided to move

Conditioning tanks at the Ring O' Bells Brewery, a 25-barrel operation

the brewery and he had the current site built over a period of eighteen months. Brewing of 25 barrels at the high-roofed, roomy brewery started in 2001 with seven beers currently being brewed regularly and at different times throughout the year.

These include the session beer Porker's Pride, a golden summer beer aimed at young lager drinkers, Surf Boar and the brewery's biggest seller Bodmin Boar, a full-flavoured malty beer. Hops used are Challenger, Goldings, Mount Hood and Styrian Goldings, the latter a favourite of Adrian because it reminds him of his honeymoon in Slovenia, which is where those hops are grown. 'I remember sitting on the edge of a hop field on a hot summer's day,' he recalls, 'and the aroma was wonderful.'

Some of the beers are pretty bitter by Westcountry standards, though there are plenty of fruity and spicy contrasts in the brews. Sales are buoyant, the beers are delicious, there are plans for bottling, and in the distant future Adrian is interested in going organic. As for Monty, sadly he passed away at the start of the summer in 2002, but his presence remains as an inspiration to the names of the Ring O' Bells' beers as well as providing a cartoonish image on the pub clips. A fine sozzled swine if ever there was.

Beers: Porker's Pride (3.8%); Surf Boar (4%); Bodmin Boar (4.3%); Dreckly (4.8%); Tipsy Trotter (5.1%); Sozzled Swine (5.5%);. Occasional: Santa's Boar (5.5%); Farmer Dray (5.5%).

Star Beer: Dreckly (4.8%) – Mid-brown, chestnut colour. On the nose there is earthy, resiny hop, with biscuity malt in the background; also some spiciness from the use of heather and gorse. Biscuity malt kicks off the tasting with a mid-palate fruitiness charging in (orange, lemon jelly, Opal Fruits); there is also more resiny hop before going into an assertive bitter-sweet finish with some malt dryness. A fruity and spicy strong ale with a very bitter finish.

Recommended outlets: The White Horse, Launceston; the Royal Inn, Horsebridge.

Roberts & Brown   Teignmouth, Devon

Brewing started off at the Teign Brewery in 1878 when the business was called William J Banbury. A name change or two later and Roberts & Co was joined by a John Deans Brown in 1900. There was stability of nomenclature until the 1920s when the company became Brown & Bishop. The end occurred in 1931 when Simonds took over the business and stopped brewing. The brewery has long been demolished and all that now remains of a business which produced beers such as A1 Ale, is the external fascia bearing the proud boast 'Teign Brewery Ales'.

Ross & Pidsley   Exeter, Devon

Brewed at the Well Park Brewery in the Alphington part of Exeter, before changing its name to Ross & Son in 1911. One of their regular beers was called Stingo, the Yorkshire term for a beer of barley wine strength. In 1913 the brewery was bought and renamed Aylwin & Snowden. In 1925 Devenish got in on the act and snapped up the company, along with its 22 pubs.

Royal Inn & Horsebridge Brewery   Horsebridge, Devon

Alongside the River Tamar, right on the Cornish border, landlord Peter Waymouth set up a small one-barrel brewery in the summer of 1982. Even though he had some of the smallest brewing kit in the country, he started off producing three different beers: Tamar Ale (OG 1039), Horsebridge Best (OG 1045) and a strong ale called Heller (OG 1060), which apparently received its name from a rude local expression. A couple of years later, the pub was sold to Terry Wood and brewing ceased for a while, but the landlord's son Simon got the mash tun working and, as well as the previous three beers, Right Royal (OG 1050) was occasionally brewed. Sadly, the pub stopped brewing its own beers in April 1999 when Simon Woods decided to move on.

The Royal Inn at Horsebridge, and some of the beers produced when it had one of the smallest breweries in the country

Landlord Paul Eaton said:

We don't turn over enough of our ale to employ another brewer. Simon wasn't just the brewer here, he was also the cellarman and general handyman. It is a great regret but we remain very much committed to real ale.

The kit was bought by Gordon Treleaven at the Driftwood Spars Hotel in St Agnes, to set up his own brewery. The Royal Inn is still a place worth visiting if you want a good pint in a lovely rural setting. It also has a chequered history. In the fifteenth century it used to be a nunnery, while during the Civil War Charles I stopped off here when it was known as the Packhorse Inn. Another notable visitor was the landscape painter JMW Turner who stayed and painted the nearby bridge.

Rye Beer

Specialist beer style which has emerged in the last few years, though there is a long-established Finnish rye-and-juniper beer called Sahti. Rye is not the easiest cereal with which to brew, as it can gum up the works in the mash tun, but O'Hanlon's, who produce a wonderful organic rye beer, get round this problem by using flakes of rye rather than grains. Rye beers are very much a small specialist niche, with O'Hanlon's the sole producer in the West Country.

Star Beer: O'Hanlon's Organic Rye Beer (5%) – A chestnut-red beer with an initial nose reminiscent of freshly baked rye bread which gives way to hints of chocolate and biscuity malt. On the palate there is a well-rounded mouthfeel, beginning with smooth chocolatey hints and maltiness, leading to a spicy, hoppy finish. This is a wonderfully complex beer with plenty going on in the nose and on the palate, leaving a delicious impression.

S *is for*
several superb local breweries...

St Anne's Well Brewery, Exeter, Devon

Brewing started in a splendid Victorian brewery built in the 1870s on the site of the stables of the Barnstaple Inn. It took its name from a source of water from nearby St Anne's Well in Sidwell Street, which had been celebrated for its curative powers from the early Middle Ages. The brewery took part in an informal merger with Norman & Pring during the Second World War, who transferred brewing to their site in the mid-1950s. St Anne's Well Brewery as a name and separate brand came to an end in 1960, but brewing continued at the site until it was closed by Whitbread in 1967. (See **Norman & Pring**.)

St Anne's Well Brewery which took its name from a holy well

St Anne's Well Brewery, Queen Street, Exeter, in 1953
Below: *Cheese tasting with Norman & Pring and St Anne's beers at Torquay in 1958*

MURRAY & CARSTAIR, TORQUAY

St Austell Brewery   St Austell, Cornwall

Several hundred years ago Cornish beer had an unimpressive reputation. One writer described it as 'looking white and thick as if pigs had wrestled in it'. Things must have improved by the middle of the nineteenth century, or else local St Austell businessman Walter Hicks would not have thought of starting up as a maltster with the eventual aim of brewing. By 1869 he had achieved his dream and was producing beer

Above: Flying the flag for Cornish ale: St Austell Brewery
Below: William Hicks, who started brewing in St Austell in 1869

for a thirsty population, many of whom worked in the local china clay industry. In 1893, the brewery was moved to newly built premises above the town, looking across St Austell Bay. The brewery was originally known as Hicks & Co but in the 1930s it was changed to St Austell. Today the magnificent brewery is still owned, and the beers still brewed, by descendants of the family. The beers are fruity, well-balanced and refreshing and can be found in over 150 brewery-owned pubs dotted throughout Cornwall and Devon, as well as in the free trade. For anyone interesting in brewing history, St Austell's 150-barrel plant and its settings are a dream.

Brewing here still works on the principles of a traditional tower brewery – just how it was planned in the nineteenth century. Work starts high up in a small room at the top, where malt is crushed by a mill after sacks are brought up by a hoist. The rest of the brewing process takes place below, with each stage being aided by gravity. The top of St Austell's on a blustery June morning is a great place to observe the process, accompanied by brewing supervisor Mervyn Westaway who has been with the company for thirty years and works closely with head brewer Roger Ryman. Mervyn explains, 'The mill is over 100 years old, and it still has to be started by hand.' He flicks a switch and the mill's belts and wheels go round, while rods pump up and down, an extremely noisy business. Down in the mash room a couple of splendid looking mash tuns with copper facings hold the grist for two of St Austell's beers, HSD and Tinners. Mervyn turns a wheel and the lid on one of the tuns rises, letting loose clouds of steam. Inside can be seen a mass of crushed, well-soaked grain from which the precious wort has been extracted. This is the second mash of the day and there is a marvellous hot cereally, almost Weetabix-like, aroma in the room.

Even though St Austell positively reeks of tradition, with lots of shining copper, brass fittings and low beams, head brewer Roger Ryman is keen to introduce new flavours and brewing techniques. Hops used for their regular beers are the English classics Fuggles and Goldings, plus the American Willamette, while speciality beers are seasoned with Cascade, Styrian Goldings and Northdown. On the way round, Mervyn Westaway shows off a small micro-brewery where Roger Ryman often comes in and plays with making different beers, usually ending up with the brewery's seasonal beers. He says:

We have a beer festival in December, and the first time we did it in 1999 we produced two novelty beers, a chocolate one called Ivan the Terrible and one called Hagar the Horrible, which was a wheat beer with cloves, coriander seeds, vanilla pods and maple syrup. Hagar was a success and we had a small amount left in bottles, so it was sent to the Tesco Spring Beer Challenge where it came top. They wanted to know the name and we had no label and didn't know where we could get the raw materials in bulk. At the time we had a beer called Red Admiral and somehow we came up with another butterfly name Clouded Yellow. It has been a big hit.

However, it is the regulars which are the bread-and-butter beers, with the full-bodied and very fruity strong ale HSD leading the pack. Meanwhile the old styles are not forgotten: St Austell produced the award-winning XXXX Mild. This has been replaced with the slightly stronger dark ale Black Prince, which has a similar taste profile to XXXX Mild. The brewery have high hopes that it will appeal to their mild drinkers. Other beers sampled at the brewery included an excellent session beer, IPA, which has a wonderful dry-hopped nose and bags of flavour and body for such a low-gravity beer, and the seasonal beer for the summer of 2002, Sunrise. This was a golden ale with malt, soft wheat and plenty of hop and fruit on the nose, with an equally fruity and hoppy character on the palate.

In common with many breweries of their vintage, in the last few years St Austell has realised the heritage value of what they do. Hence the fascinating visitor centre which celebrates the rich history of the

St Austell's micro-brewery where the champion wheat beer Clouded Yellow was conceived, using vanilla pods, maple syrup, cloves and coriander seeds, as well as the usual ingredients of beer

Above: *Mash tun at St Austell*
Right: *St Austell's head brewer Roger Ryman at the mash tun – he joined the brewery in 1999 from Scottish brewers Maclays*

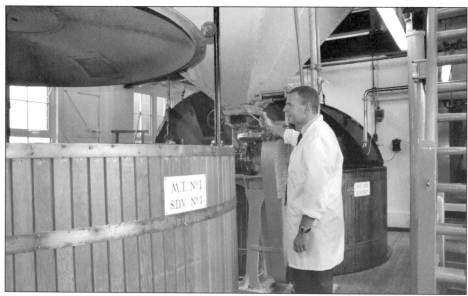

Racking casks of beer at St Austell – it is at this stage where finings are added to help the yeast settle; it is also now when a small amount of hops are added to St Austell's IPA, a process known as dry-hopping

brewery, including a roll call of former beers such as the barley wines Smuggler's and Prince's Ale, sadly no longer made. This is also the starting and finishing point for all brewery tours. If you are interested in following the trail of Westcountry ales, this is an essential stopping-off point. (See **HSD, Wheat Beer.**)

Beers: IPA (3.4%); Tinners Ale (3.7%); Black Prince (4%); Dartmoor Best Bitter (3.9%); Tribute (4.2%); HSD (5%). Occasional: four seasonal beers. In 2002 the brewery produced Wind Jammer (4.3%), Trelawny's (4.1%); Sunrise (3.9%) and Cockle Roaster (4.7%). Bottles: Tribute, HSD, Clouded Yellow, the latter is bottle-conditioned; in 2001 the brewery also produced a limited edition commemorative bottle-conditioned 1851 (10.2%), while the following year saw a bottle-conditioned Golden Jubilee Ale (6.3%).

Star Beer: Tribute (4.2%) – Originally released as eclipse beer Daylight Robbery in 1999, it proved such a hit that it became a regular. Amber in colour, the nose has bags of citrus fruit and hops. On the palate there is an initial taste of biscuity malt before citrus fruit and hops burst on to the scene, leading to a long bitter and zesty finish which also has a hint of malt. Very fruity and hoppy though balanced by a good fresh maltiness. Very drinkable.

Recommended outlets: The Fountain Inn, Newbridge near Penzance; the Star Inn, St Just-in-Penwith.

St Giles in the Wood   Great Torrington, Devon

Publican Steve Lock set up a small brewery in an industrial unit in 1998. The equipment came from Sutton Brewery in Plymouth and two beers were produced, Best Bitter (4.2%) and Premium (5.3%). Brewing lasted only until 1999, when the kit and industrial unit were bought by Brian Broughton who set up Clearwater.

Scattor Rock Brewery   Christow, Devon

Christow, with its thatched white-walled cottages, is home to Scattor Rock Brewery, based on a small industrial estate at the edge of the village in the Teign Valley. It is a compact four-barrel brewery set up in 1998 by Keith Stanaway who used to work in banking before taking an early retirement package. He felt too young to spend all his time on the golf course, however, and when micro-brewing was suggested to him as a business opportunity it was all hands to the mash tun. He says:

It was built up completely from scratch with no customers and no equipment. This space was empty and we had to design it ourselves with the help of a consultant. I knew nothing about it, and I mainly drink red wine, but it seemed like a good idea.

Scattor Rock Brewery

The brewery was named after a local landmark at a nearby quarry site. The quarry closed by 1950 with the remaining part of the tor being blown up. With the passage of time the name 'Scattor Rock' was slowly being forgotten and we felt it appropriate to name the brewery after this once famous tor. We wanted a local flavour to things, and because we are on Dartmoor and the names of the beers are linked to tors – it generates a lot of interest.

Malt comes from Tuckers Maltings, while hops are both English and from all over the world, including America, Canada and New Zealand. Brewer Phil White, a native of Newton Abbot, has been with the operation from the beginning:

We spent the day with a brewing consultant and he gave me relevant diagrams and I went away and built the brewing kit. He came when we did our first brew, but all the equipment had just been delivered. As the brew went through I was still putting pieces together. As we carried on brewing I was tweaking things and just kept playing around to get it right.

Even though he describes his beers as fairly hoppy, but not as bitter as northern beers, Phil is something of a hop demon. English hops are mainly used in the regular beers which have a good malt and hop balance, with plenty of underlying fruitiness. However, with the specials, of which there are three a month, he goes to the hop market with a vengeance.

Over the years he reckons he has used 30 different hop varieties from all over the world, with one of his favourites being a New Zealand one called Green Bullet. 'From day one hops have come from Charles Faram,' he says. 'They would send a brochure and we would try all the different hops they had.' These special beers are also Phil's chance to play around with beer styles and produce a few beers out of the ordinary. In his all-year selection you will find a lager, a mild, seasonal beers and dark beers such as Scattor Brain and Night Porter. These are Phil's favourites. 'Both are dark beers for the winter months, with Scattor Brain aiming to be a Cotleigh Old Buzzard style of beer, while Night Porter is more of a strong mild.' Grandaddy of all Scattor Rock's beers must be Completely and Utterly Brain Dead which weighs in at a stupendous 9% – not recommended if you plan an assault on one of the local tors.

Beers: Scatty Bitter (3.8%); Teign Valley Tipple (4%); Sky Lark (4.2%); Devonian (4.5%); Golden Valley (4.6%); Valley Stomper (5%). Occasional: Hound Tor Reserve (4.8%); Farmer Lightfoot (3.7%); Rippon Tor Extra (4.5%); Scotch Ale (4.5%); Scattor Brain (5.2%); Hay Tor Porter (4.3%); Swell Tor (5%); Cluster Bomb (4.8%); Yes Tor (4.1%); Kingfisher (5.2%); Quarryman Stout (4.4%); Shelstone Tor (4.3%); Brent Tor Mild (3.8%); Golden Gorse (5.1%); Cox Tor (3.9%); Same Again (4.1%); Bellever Tor Honey Ale (4.6%); Steeperton Tor (4.2%); Gidley's Bitter (Anniversary Ale) (4.4%); Lynch Tor Premium (4.7%); Steeperton Tor (4.2%); Augustus (4.6%); Corndon Tor Original (4.3%); Scary Tor (4.5%); The King Evil (6%); Sittaford Tor Stout (4.9%); Night Porter (5.2%); Completely and Utterly Brain Dead (9%); Dinger Tor Delight (4.8%); Ten Tors Award Ale (5.1%); Scattor Brain (5.2%); Scattor Claus (4.7%).

Star Beer: Lynch Tor Premium (4.7%) – Malt-accented golden bitter with a hoppy nose. On the palate there is a strong malt presence at the start and in the finish, but this is more than balanced by a fruity, citrusy hoppiness which emerges mid-palate and continues through the long, bitter finish.

Recommended outlets: Teign House Inn, Christow; Bridford Inn, Bridford.

Secondary Fermentation

Primary fermentation occurs during the brewing process when yeast is pitched into the hopped wort. Next stage is racking into casks, and with real ale there is always enough residual yeast for a secondary fermentation to continue, developing the flavour and condition of the beer. Secondary fermentation, therefore, is an essential part of cask-conditioned or real ale. (See **Brewing**.)

Sharp's   Rock, Cornwall

After the ales of St Austell, the most common beers to be found in the pubs of Cornwall and Devon are those of Sharp's. Set up in 1994 by former silversmith and farmer Bill Sharp in the quaintly named Pityme industrial estate, the brewery has undergone a phenomenal growth in the last few years. It started off with brewing ten barrels a week and expanded very rapidly. Within a year it was even supplying beer to the

House of Commons. Nowadays, it supplies over 300 outlets in Cornwall and further afield, which means that the 50-barrel brewery was once more undergoing expansion during the summer of 2002. Bottling is also planned with Doom Bar Bitter and Sharp's Own the most likely candidates. Sales manager James Nicholls says:

We took off because of the quality of the product, and the consistency of that quality. We also make sure we use quality ingredients, and we pride ourselves on the quality of backup and service we can give to customers.

Sharp's started with two beers, Sharp's Own and Cornish Coaster, which were followed by the likes of Doom Bar Bitter and Special. Currently there are six beers being produced throughout the year by the brewery, their names reflecting their Cornish birthplace and plays on Bill Sharpe's name; Will's Resolve, for instance, was closely associated with the Millennium having been brewed for the 1999 eclipse, when it was named Elevenses. There is also Eden Ale, especially brewed for the Eden Project, winner of the Supreme Champion award at the Falmouth Beer Festival in 2000. The brewery also produces blended 'house beers' for a few Cornish pubs, including the Maltsters Arms at Chapel Amble and the Countryman at Piece near Redruth. Apparently, the beer for the latter got the name No-Name due to the locals being unable to come up with a suitable name.

Flavourwise, they are well-balanced beers with a well-rounded maltiness and a fruity, floral hoppiness. There is also a slight hint of sweetness in the finish. You could even say that they have set the benchmark for a whole host of Cornish beers which have followed since. As to what makes their beers so drinkable, that is a mystery as Sharp's are known for keeping their brewing secrets to themselves. Whatever the hops are (and it is a fair guess that they are quite familiar ones), these are delicious beers which stay Sharp to the bottom of the glass.

Beers: Cornish Coaster (3.6%); Doom Bar Bitter (4%); Eden Ale (4.2%); Own (4.4%); Will's Resolve (4.6%); Special Ale (5.2%); bottles: Eden Ale.
Star beer: Sharp's Own (4.4%) – A dark-amber best bitter with a very fruity nose which also packs in bubblegum, Seville orange and rich marmalade straight out of the jar; there is also a trace of biscuit malt,

but the nose is definitely fruit and hop orientated. On the palate there is good biscuity malt, before a citrusy and hoppy character takes over leading into lasting, if not too pronounced, hoppy bitterness which also retains the fruitiness of the palate.

Recommended outlets: The Blue Peter, Polperro; the Old Success, Sennen Cove.

SIBA

Otherwise known as the Society of Small Independent Brewers, whose years of campaigning for smaller brewers to pay less duty on their beers came to fruition in the budget of 2002. SIBA also organises various beer festivals, with SIBA South West's showcase being the Maltings Beer Festival in Newton Abbot. SIBA members in Devon also organise a beer tent at the Devon Show in May.

Skinner's Brewery   Truro, Cornwall

Before setting up Skinner's in 1997, Steve and Sarah Skinner used to live in Jersey. They were in the licensing trade for years and started their own brew-pub in the early-1990s, the Tipsy Toad. By the mid-1990s, they were looking for a change of lifestyle and considered setting up a brewery in Ireland, France or Cornwall. The latter eventually won, with no small thanks due to the excellence of Cornish waters for surfing, which is a real passion of the Skinner family (apart from Sarah, that is, who says that she dislikes cold water). In fact, the surfing bug is shared by most of the brewery, with prospective employees always being quizzed about surfing when they are interviewed. The first Skinner's beers started trundling out in July 1997 and rapidly found an appreciative local market. Awards also followed with Cornish Knocker winning Supreme Champion at the Tuckers

Above: *Skinner's Brewery, with the unique copper which originally came from a whisky distillery*
Left: *Skinner's head brewer Will Freeland checking the hop quality – a wonderful hoppy character is a mainstay of the beers Will produces*

Skinner's Brewery: a fermenting vessel with Betty Stogs Bitter – an award-winning beer which is named after a character from Cornish folklore

Maltings festival in 1998 and Betty Stoggs Bitter doing the same the following year.

A large part of the success of the beers can be put down to the fact that they are clean-tasting, well-balanced and with a delicious fruity and hoppy character. Hops used are Northdown, Styrian Goldings, Challenger, Cascade and Mount Hood. 'We produce what people want to drink,' says head brewer Will Freeland who worked with Steve and Sarah in Jersey before linking up with them when they were established in Truro. He is a graduate in marine and fish biology, but his membership of the 'Let's Sit Down and Drink Beer and Talk about Whales Society' at college might have given some indication of a future career path. The brewery is a 25-barrel operation with up to six brews a week occurring; intriguingly, the copper used to be an old whisky still. There are six regular beers, all named after Cornish folklore figures and boasting colourful, comic-book style pumpclips and beer labels. They give a sense of youth and liveliness to the brewery's image which has probably helped them reach out to drinkers who might not always think of real ale.

Betty Stogs Bitter is the best-seller, a hoppy best bitter which celebrates the eponymous Betty, an ale-loving, lazy good-for-nothing who reformed herself after the little people took her child away from her for a good wash in the morning dew. As for the popular Cornish Knocker, this got its name from a small tourist gift which Sarah had been given, as she explains:

When we started we wanted an imagery for the beers which was different, not the normal run-of-the-mill names. A friend of mine in Jersey has given

"Betty Stoggs was a native of West Cornwall. She was unkempt and lazy, could never mend her stockings, couldn't knit or cook and liked a drop of ale. Her child was taken from her by the "small people" washed in the morning dew and returned. The shock of which turned Betty into a reformed character. Sort of!!"

WWW.SKINNERSBREWERY.COM — CORNISH FOLKLORE –

me a 'freshly caught fairy', which was a jam jar with a fairy inside poking out its head from blades of grass. When we were unpacking after the move the jar turned up and we noticed that it said it was a Cornish Knocker. Something clicked, we started researching Cornish history and the names started to come.

The future is bright for Skinner's. In a few years they have become one of the South West's most successful breweries. They own two pubs and would like more in the right circumstances, while there are also plans to move their site, by the side of the Truro River, to something a bit bigger. Meanwhile, surfing competitions and Cornish rugby's major trophy are sponsored. Skinner's obviously have the little people on their side.

Beers: Coastliner (3.4%); Spriggan Ale (3.8%); Betty Stogs Bitter (4%); Figgy's Brew (4.5%); Cornish Knocker (4.5%); Cornish Blonde (5%) – there is also an extra cold one called Ice Blonde (5%). Occasional: Bishop Bill's Truro Brew (4.8%); Mild Oatmeal Stout (4%); Heligan Honey (4%); Jingle Knockers (5.5%). Bottles: Heligan Honey; Cornish Knocker; Cornish Blonde, Jingle Knockers; Bishop Bill's Truro Brew.

Star Beer: Betty Stogs Bitter (4%) – Amber to chestnut-brown best bitter with a sprightly hop fruitiness on the nose – almost reminscent of fruit jelly. On the palate there is an introduction of grainy, chewy maltiness which quickly gives way to a delicious hop fruitiness with hints of passion fruit. The finish is dry and bitter with the fruitiness echoing away. Very quaffable.

Recommended outlets: Skinner's Ale House, Newquay; the Quayside, Falmouth.

Smoked Beer

Prior to the Industrial Revolution and the discovery of coke, malt was cured over wood or coal fires. In the cities, coal was banned for kilning and so wood was used, which led to beers that were brewed with brown malt having a smoky edge. After coke was discovered, malting techniques improved, and smoked beer became a Bavarian speciality centred on the city of Bamberg. However, the last few years have seen a few British brewers experimenting with smoked beers and no doubt the West Country will one day be home to one.

Society of Preservation of Beers from the Wood

Before CAMRA, there was the SPBW who emerged in 1963 with the aim of saving wooden casks. However, as Richard Boston pointed out in the classic book *Beer And Skittles*, their aims were a little misguided:

Wooden casks are picturesque, and give better temperature insulation than metal ones. Otherwise they are rather a nuisance to all concerned: to the publican because they are so heavy, and to the brewer because they are hard to sterilise and therefore more liable to infection.

Despite being eclipsed by CAMRA the SPBW is still going, possibly offering an optional social club to devoted beer drinkers.

South Devon Brewery   Kingsbridge, Devon

Based at Union Road, the company was known as WH Prowse & Sons until 1946. It was not a good augury for the future as brewing was halted a couple of years later and the whole operation, including 25 pubs, was bought up by Simonds, who had already purchased Crake's in Plymouth.

Stallion Ales   Helland

Originally based near Chippenham, Stallion Ales moved to Bodmin and began brewing in late 1985, with two beers: Stallion (OG 1040) and Barnstormer (OG 1060). Another beer, Riding Ale (OG 1046) was added to the range but despite being available in local pubs brewing stopped in 1987.

Starkey, Knight & Ford   Tiverton, Devon

Originally Somerset-based, this brewery gained a foothold (and an extra name) in Devon in 1895 when they purchased Thomas Ford & Son in Tiverton. Thomas Ford started brewing in 1852 at Westexe North, but five years later he had set up at a site which is now taken by Tesco's. Breweries in Barnstaple, Paignton, Sidmouth and Uffculme (Furze's Steam Brewery) were also taken over in the following decades while 'Tivvy ales' became a popular selling slogan; a bottled beer Tivvy Brown Ale was produced up until the early-1970s. In the early-1960s, Whitbread stepped in and took over the whole business. Whitbread apparently had plans to build a new mega-brewery serving the South West on an industrial estate at Exeter, but instead built a bottling and canning plant a mile away from the original brewery in Tiverton. The operation was renamed Whitbread Flowers and closed in 1982.

Stock Ale

Very strong beers which were also known as keeping beers. Usually they are only produced in the winter months and laid down to mature for a long time, with the large amount of alcohol stopping the beers from ruin. They have all but died out, but Teignworthy do produce Edwin Tucker's Victorian Stock Ale (12%) in limited supplies every year. It is brewed in October and Teignworthy's John Lawton recommends that the bottles be allowed to mature for a few years before drinking.

Star Beer: Edwin Tucker's Victorian Stock Ale (12%) – Very dark in colour, with a breathtaking alcoholic and malty nose followed by plenty of stewed fruit and dark chocolate. On the palate, there is a

Edwin Tucker's Victorian Stock Ale, a survivor from the days of Queen Victoria, and a beer to be laid down like a fine wine

smooth mouthfeel with plenty of rich malt, more alcohol and bitterness from the hops. The finish is warming, malty and slightly fruity. A classic, and a beer to be respected.

Stout

A drop of the black usually means Guinness but the last few years have seen many small breweries producing stouts. These are dark and delicious beers packed with flavour, aroma and a stupendous, lip-smacking finish. Many drinkers consider them to be infinitely superior to the mass-produced stouts which are often chilled to the point of tastelessness. The origin of stout lies in the porter revolution of the eighteenth century. The strongest porters were called stout porters and eventually the two beers became separated. Porter died out for many years and has only made a comeback in the last couple of decades, but stout has gone from strength to strength. Part of the appeal of stout is the use of roast barley in the mash which gives it its dry and roasted palate; it is a similar tasting experience to a good espresso. There is also a good rate of hopping for the finish. Some breweries used to make oyster stouts, with a small amount of oyster extract added; a very rare sight these days. Westcountry breweries making stout include Sutton, O'Hanlon's, the Organic Brewhouse, Points West and Skinner's, whose Mild Oatmeal Stout is delicious. (See **Double Stout, Entire, Milk Stout, Porter**.)

Star Stout: O'Hanlon's Port Stout (4.8%) – Black-coloured with a dark-brown tinge. A nose of roast barley, roast coffee beans with subtle hints of smokiness and vanilla, leads to an initially creamy mouthfeel with some fruitiness, followed by a stupendous dry, bitter finish which is balanced by the sweetest hint of port.

Based on an old Irish hangover cure, O'Hanlon's Original Port Stout is a unique and intriguing stout which has won many awards

Summerskills Brewery   Billacombe, Plymouth, Devon

Never mix the grape with the grain is what the old folks say, but in 1983 that did not stop wine-maker Adam Summerskill from setting up a two-barrel brewery on his vineyard near Bigbury Bay in South Devon. Its striking logo, still in use, features an upright arm holding an armour-clad leg. This apparently was the sign of a local nobleman, which was also used as a ship's crest by HMS *Bigbury Bay*. A year later, with Bigbury Best Bitter (OG 1042) under his belt, Adam Summerskill moved the brewery to its current home on an industrial estate outside Plymouth. Brewing capacity was increased to ten barrels, with kit coming from the closed Penrhos Brewery which had been set up by Monty Python comedian Terry Jones. 'The local council was against us expanding our brewery in its present rural setting,' said Adam Summerskill at the time, 'so we are moving.' However, the brewery was put into mothballs in 1985 and that seemed the end of things. After several years along came former hotelier Rick Wilson and ex-Navy man Carl Beeson, who in 1990 bought the plant and resurrected the Summerskills name. Carl recalls:

The Tardis-like interior of Summerskills, showing the mill (left) with which they crush their own malt

'Rick had sold his hotel, didn't have a job and fancied a change, and I was made redundant from my job in the food industry,' says Carl, who apparently has been to known to spend his summer weekends charging around the countryside as a member of the Sealed Knot re-enactment society.

We both liked beer and thought why not make a go of it. We started with one beer, Best Bitter, and went round different pubs trying to sell it and it grew by word and mouth. A year after we started we did another beer.

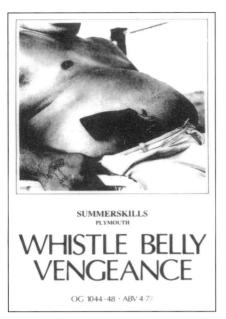

SUMMERSKILLS
PLYMOUTH

WHISTLE BELLY VENGEANCE

OG 1044-48 · ABV 4.7%

Summerskills Brewery's Whistle Belly Vengeance, which whetted the whistles of the nation's MPs

Since then Summerskills have gained a name for beers such as the exotically named Whistle Belly Vengeance, which has been on sale in the House of Commons bar, and the rich dark winter warmer Indiana's Bones. Rick brews three times a week, using malt from Tuckers Maltings and English hops, including Goldings. The actual brewery is akin to Dr Who's Tardis. From the outside it looks tiny, but inside there is all the paraphenalia of brewing packed into a compact space. They even mill their own malt, a rare event for small breweries. There are four regular beers, with several more coming on-stream during the winter. 'Our beers are not over-hoppy,' says Carl. 'We have been told by some of the old boys that our Best Bitter tastes a bit like Plymouth Breweries' Best Bitter.' Carl is also a former South-West SIBA chairman and is credited with coming up with the idea for the Tuckers Maltings festival back in the early-1990s and has fond memories of some of the earlier festivals:

I thought why don't we put on a festival run by and for brewers, something where we could be exhibiting our beers. I remember one mayor of Newton Abbot who went on a tour of the town's pubs with a bunch of landlords. By the time he arrived at the festival the only thing that was keeping his coat on was the mayoral chain.

Beers: Cellar Vee (3.7%); Hop Scotch (4.1%); Best Bitter (4.3%); Tamar Best Bitter (4.3%); Whistle Belly Vengeance (4.7%); Indiana Bones (5.6%). Occasional beers: O'Summerskills Shamrock Stout (4.4%); Ninjabeer (5%); Turkey's Delight (5.1%). Bottled: Whistle Belly Vengeance, bottle-conditioned.

Star Beer: Whistle Belly Vengeance (4.7%) – Reddish-brown colour, assertive malty nose plus hints of resiny hoppiness; malty and hints of chocolate in the background to start with; mid-palate a subtle citrusy fruitiness kicks in; there is a good bitterness in the finish which also has rounded maltiness. Beautifully crafted beer which is more malty than hoppy.

Recommended pubs: Prince Maurice, Eggbuckland, Plymouth; Ship Inn, Noss Mayo.

Sutton Brewery   Plymouth, Devon

At the tail-end of the 1980s Quintin and Debra Style were tenants at a Courage pub in Plymouth. Quintin was a native South African who had once served as a paratrooper during the Angolan wars in the 1970s, while Debra was originally from Scotland but had moved with her family to South Africa as a teenager. They had fetched up in Plymouth. What they really wanted was their own place, while Quintin dreamt of setting up a small brewery alongside. On their nights off they would

Sutton Brewery, who returned brewing to Plymouth in a regenerated former industrial area, which also boasts an aquarium and marina

The mark of a good pint: Sutton Brewery's striking sign which can be found at the front of the Thistle Park Brewhouse

Inside the Sutton Brewery, where head brewer Ben Ridgeon brews the likes of Knickadroppa Glory and XSB

wander over to the Thistle Park Tavern, an imposing Victorian public house in the Coxside part of Plymouth, not far from Sutton harbour. The area was once a hive of industry and there used to be a railway alongside the Tavern. There was also a nearby park full of thistles, which is how the Tavern came by its name. Now it is a regenerated area of tidy terraced cottages with a marina, aquarium and leisure complex nearby. But back in the late-1980s, there was a space next to the pub where someone was trying to set up a small engineering works. Quintin would say to Debra that if they owned the pub he would also buy that space, which is where they would build their brewery. They bought the pub in 1988, and in 1993 the dream became reality: the Sutton Brewery began brewing.

Initially it was a five-barrel operation but as it became busier it increased to ten barrels, still the same today, with brewing taking place three times a week. Ben Ridgeon is the head brewer, a job he had been doing for a year at the time of writing. In his early-twenties, he must be one of the youngest head brewers in the business. A local lad, he was always interested in real ale and after working in pubs in London became interested in brewing. After helping out at Sutton for a couple of years, he got his chance with the mash tun when the previous brewer Steve Cheeseright went to work at the Nursery Brewery in Bristol.

The core of Sutton Brewery's beers are Plymouth Pride; XSB ('our flag-ship beer,' says Ben, 'the first we ever made'), Sutton Comfort and the award-winning Knickadroppa Glory, whose pumpclip features a rather risqué drawing. Seasonal beers include Wild Blonde, Plymouth Porter and a strong Christmas ale Sleigh'd. Other beers are occasionally brewed, including one that uses orange juice and peel in the brew,

Orangatang. In the hop department, Ben only uses two: Brambling Cross, which sometimes gives a hint of blackcurrant to a beer, as well as a warm hop spiciness, and the supremely aromatic American hop Cascade. The beers go out to over 50 pubs, but Sutton has a definite advantage in that the pub next door (now called the Thistle Park Brewhouse) always stocks at least four of the brewery's beers. In a city which has lost its brewing tradition over the years and seen most of its pubs tied to Courage or pub chains, Sutton Brewery and the Thistle Park Brewhouse provide great beers and a wonderful place in which to drink them.

Beers: Plymouth Pride (3.8%); XSB (4.2%); Sutton Comfort (4.5%); Knickadroppa Glory (5.5%). Occasional: Grommet (3.8%); Wild Blonde (4.4%); Bump In The Night (4.5%); Orangatang (4.8%); Pandamonium (4.8%); Plymouth Porter (5%). Bottles: Madiba Stout (5%); Knickadroppa Glory; all bottle-conditioned.

Star Beer: Knickadroppa Glory (5.5%) – Chestnut-brown strong ale with a good firm roasted malt nose, intertwined with dried fruit, currants and chocolate malt. On the nose there are also toffee hints from the crystal malt and a hop fruitiness also coming through as the beer develops in the glass. On the palate there is a lot of roast maltiness balanced by citric fruitiness leading to a long, dry, bitter finish. Great characterful beer which is very moreish for its strength.

Recommended pubs: Miners Arms, Hemerdon; Hope and Anchor, Hope Cove.

Swayne & Co   Torquay, Devon

Business was started by the Swayne brothers in the late-nineteenth century, who brewed at Fleet Street. At the beginning of 1900 they moved to the Ellacombe Brewery in Lower Ellacombe. In 1925 they were bought by Plymouth Breweries who also got their hands on fellow Torquay brewers Greenslade Brothers in the same year.

Sweetness

Beers in the West Country were reckoned to be sweeter than those elsewhere in England. After all, what would you expect from the area of cream teas and clotted cream? 'People here like sweet things,' says John Lawton at Teignworthy, 'my father hated the local beer when he was stationed here in the Army. He liked it dry and hoppy.'

Swimbridge Brewery   Swimbridge, Devon

After seventeen years working as second brewer at Wadworth's of Devizes, Jeff Patton joined forces with three other real ale enthusiasts to bring real beer to North Devon. Brewing started in August 1981 in an old tannery, which was fitted out with a brand-new ten-barrel kit and

Swayne's Ellacombe Brewery at Torquay, photographed in 1985

'all the scientific quality control checks that you will find in a large brewery', according to finance manager John Moulton. The first beer was Swimbridge Bitter (OG 1038), a standard session beer with plenty of bitterness. The brewery went into liquidation a couple of years later with Jeff Patton laying the blame for the demise on tough trading conditions: 'We had to face competition from the big brewers, not over the quality of our beer but over offering discounts.'

T *is for*
taste, tavern and Tally Ho...

Tally Ho Brewery   Hatherleigh, Devon

When this traditional inn started to produce beers from a small 3.5-barrel brewing kit at the start of the 1990s, it revived a tradition which stretched back to the eighteenth century. It had stopped in the early-1900s when the then owners decided they could no longer cope with demand for national brands. The new beers were brewed at the back of the premises in what used to be the town bakery, and included Master Jack's Mild (3.4%), Potboilers Brew (3.5%), Market Ale (3.7%), Tarka's Tipple (4%), Nutters (4.6%) and Midnight Madness (5%). There was also a winter warmer, Jollop (6.8%), which was strong and comforting, with a good malt character and an excellent hoppy finish, plus a bottled-conditioned product called Thurgia (5.7%). Other special bottled beers were produced for special events. These were well-crafted, flavoursome beers which could be enjoyed in a wonderful bar with low wooden beams, a log fire in the winter and excellent food. However, this is all in the past now as brewing of the Tally Ho ales came to a halt in 2001 and from reports received it does not look likely to restart. However, it is still a great pub to visit.

The Tally Ho, Hatherleigh, where a pint of Nutters was a standard tipple until brewing came to an end in 2001

Above: Bar scene at the Tally Ho in the 1990s
Above right: The Tally Ho Brewery during the 1990s

The Tamar Brewery, Plymouth, formerly home to Crake's, and bought by Courage in 1960, photo taken in 1985

Tamar Brewery   Devonport, Devon

The brewery was originally home to C Crake, who started up in the 1820s. Nearly a century later Crake's was bought up by Simonds. Brewing continued at the site with a name change under the auspices of Simonds until they, in turn, merged with Courage in 1960. The brewery finally stopped production in 1975 when it was sold to the MOD for dockyard extensions, though some of the plant ended up with Blackawton, the first of the new wave of small breweries to start up in Devon in the 1970s.

Tasting

Tasting beer starts with looking. The beer should be clear (unless it is a wheat beer style) and you can also judge the conditioning by seeing how lively it is. A tired beer lacks sparkle and is almost dull; it will leave no trace of lacework on the glass as you drink it. Swirl the beer around as this helps to release its aromas. Note the colour which is a result of the various malts used. Then, aroma. One of the great joys of a beer is the aroma. Malt aromas include dried fruit, coffee, Ovaltine, plain chocolate, toffee and caramel. Hoppy aromas are fruity, resiny, aromatic, perfumey, peppery, citric and floral. Thirdly, taste. The human tongue is a delicate instrument which detects sweetness at the tip, salt and sour on the side and bitter at the back of the tongue. Let the beer wash over your tongue and try to guess the flavour sensations you pick up. Malt can produce a chewy, biscuity, grainy, toasty flavour; it also hints at currants, Dundee cake, nuts, chocolate, toffee or coffee beans. It can also give dryness to the finish of the beer. Hops have a flowery, citrusy, resiny, peppery or aromatic effect on the palate; bitterness is also a hop by-product. On the palate hops also suggest Seville oranges, marmalade, blackcurrants, lychees, grapefruit and even fruit jelly babies. Fruity aromas and tastes, especially in stronger beers, are sometimes also a result of the yeast at work.

If you have the luck to enter the yeast room of a good brewery be prepared to be enchanted by the fruitiness which comes with good English ale. Do swallow the beer when tasting. Unlike wine tasting where you can spit all day long, part of beer tasting involves letting the beer work its effect on your throat. In classic English bitters we can feel dryness and bitterness. A great beer will be well-balanced; the malt and hops should work together rather than overwhelm each other. Also note the beer's finish, does it make you want another? It should. Go on, pour yourself another. (See **Flavour**.)

Tavern
While inns served food and drink to travellers, taverns traditionally offered the same services to town dwellers. The heyday of the tavern was during the seventeenth and eighteenth centuries, when they became a home from home to the likes of Dr Johnson and Samuel Pepys. Nowadays, tavern is a phrase, like inn, which is sometimes used for a pub with pretensions.

Teignworthy Newton Abbot, Devon
Warwickshire-born John Lawton wanted to be a farmer and so came down to an agricultural college near Newton Abbot. It soon dawned on him that he would not achieve his own farm without a serious input of cash which led him to taking his first steps into brewing for a living. Like his father, he was a home-brewer, and this experience was to stand him in great stead when he spent the summer of 1988 at Ringwood in Hampshire. After that he brewed in Derby and Somerset, before setting up Teignworthy in 1993. He recalls:

Teignworthy's John Lawton with Tuckers Maltings' Richard Wheeler in the germination room

Teignworthy Brewery, which John and Rachel Lawton set up in the summer of 1993

I enjoyed my time at Oakhill in Somerset but I still wanted to do my own thing. When I was at college I used to get my malt for home-brewing from Tuckers Maltings and asked its director, Richard Wheeler, if he could help with finding somewhere. Tuckers said yes very quickly and suggested a space at the Maltings. In the meantime Rachel and I were married in the spring, moved down here and within a month we had all the equipment and people in. We were brewing in June.

Teignworthy is in a unique position at the historic Tuckers Maltings which is one of a handful of traditional floor maltings left in the country. It might not have a beautiful view of the sea or high moor but, on the other hand, it is based where beer starts its journey from malted barley to the glass in your hand. The 15-barrel plant is organised on the principle of a tower brewery, where everything works by the aid of gravity. Part of the brewery features in the official tour of the Maltings, so you are likely to catch a glimpse of John checking things, or one of the brewery's workers pitching yeast into the beer ready to be fer-

Teignworthy Brewery's Harvey's Special Brew, brewed to celebrate the birth of John and Rachel's son Harvey; all three Lawton children now have beers named after them

mented. There are two full-time and three part-time staff, including Derek Newman, who was a judge at the Tuckers Maltings Beer Festival, resplendent in a three-cornered hat, a robe and chain of office. He is Newton Abbot's portreeve, a bit like a beagle or a town crier without the handbell-ringing and oyezing.

Six of Teignworthy Brewery's specially brewed beers standing in the germinating room at Tuckers Maltings

This is not the place to come for exotic fruit beers or curious brews where vanilla pods or arcane spices are an essential part of the tasting experience. 'I like to make something that people drink and enjoy,' says John. 'I'm not trying to be extreme. I aim to please pub-goers.'

There are four regulars which use the hops Brambling Cross, Goldings, Fuggles and Challenger in different combinations. These include Reel Ale (4%), so named because of John's love for fishing, and Springtime (4.3%), a well-rounded best bitter with plenty of malt and fruit on the palate leading to a dry, fruity finish with a hint of sweetness. John also produces several seasonal ales, including three named after his young children. He is a busy man. As well as producing his own beers, he works with Brian Gates from the Tuckers Maltings beer shop to produce a series of unique beers based on old recipes researched by Brian and released in bottle under the name Edwin Tucker. No wonder he despairs of ever going fishing again. (See **Arctic Ale, Imperial Russian Porter, IPA, Stock Ale, Tuckers Maltings.**)

Beers: Reel Ale (4%); Springtime (4.3%); Old Moggy (4.4%); Beachcomber (4.5%). Occasional: Making Ends Meet (3.8%); Harvey's Special Brew (4.6%); Amy's Ale (4.8%); Maltsters Ale (5%); Christmas Cracker (6%). Bottles: Reel Ale; Springtime; Old Moggy; Beachcomber; Harvey's Special Brew; Amy's Ale; Maltsters Ale; Martha's Mild (5.3%); Christmas Cracker; Edwin Tucker's Maris Otter (5.5%); Edwin Tucker's East India Pale Ale (6.5%); Edwin Tucker's Devonshire Strong Ale (8%); Coffin Polish Stronger Elixer (8.4%); Edwin Tucker's Arctic Ale (9%); Edwin Tucker's Empress Russian Porter (10.5%); Edwin Tucker's Victorian Stock Ale (12%); all bottle-conditioned.

Star Beer: Reel Ale (4%) – Light-brown in colour with plenty of fruity and hoppy aromas on the nose. There is also a hint of biscuit malt. On the palate, the biscuity maltiness kicks in immediately before a fruity (oranges) and hoppy mid-palate joins the fray. The finish is bitter and dry with elements of fruitiness lingering for a short time. Harmony between the malt and hop makes this a well-balanced, clean-tasting, fruity session beer.

Recommended pubs: Railway Inn, Whiddon Down Road, North Tawton; New Fountain Inn, Whimple.

Thompson's Brewery   London Hotel, Ashburton, Devon

In 1981 Danny Thompson and his son Melvyn set up a small three-barrel brewery in the upstairs bar of the London Hotel, an old coaching inn. Most of the equipment was home-made and their first beer was Aysheburton Bitter (OG 1040), later to be called Best Bitter, which they offered for sale in two-pint mugs. The other beers brewed were a Mild (OG 1033) and an IPA (OG 1045) – one writer called it a strong bitter which 'crept up on the unwary'. Expansion followed early in 1992 with a larger brewing capacity (the brewery moving into the pub's converted stables), and the beer range increased over the years. By the mid-1990s, Thompson's was offering an eclectic range of ales, in addition to the best bitter and IPA, including a mild brewed especially for CAMRA's twenty-first anniversary (3.6%), Black Velvet Stout (4.2%), Figurehead (5.1%), a fruity copper-red beer, a golden summer beer Man Of War (5.2%), a Christmas beer called Yuletide Tipple (5.3%) and a Celebration Porter (6%), which in later years was reduced to 4%.

Above: *The London Inn, Ashburton, home of Thompson's Brewery until 1997, when a fire damaged the hotel*
Above right: *Handpumps at Thompson's with a promise of their IPA and Best Bitter*

For a short while not long before closure, a session beer, Lunchtime Bitter (3.4%), was brewed. In 1990, the brewery owned three tied houses, including the Mutton Cove Tavern in Devonport, but it soon concentrated on the one pub in Ashburton while getting its beer out into the free trade in Devon. Despite a variety of outlets, brewing came to an end in 1997 about six months after a fire badly damaged the hotel, which never reopened and was subsequently sold to a local builder along with the brewery. All of the equipment was quickly sold on.

Tower Brewery

Style of brewery, usually built in the nineteenth century, where the brewing process started at the top and carried on in stages downwards, thus letting gravity do all the hard work. Malt was usually hoisted up to the top where it was milled. Down below was the hot liquor tank and mash tun. Below this was the copper and finally, at the bottom, the fermenting vessels and conditioning tanks. Under this system it was possible to contain all the brewing operations in a compact site. Apart from St Austell, a working tower brewery is a rare sight these days, though several smaller breweries such as Teignworthy have their brewery organised on the tower brewery style. (See **Brewing**.)

Tuckers Maltings   Newton Abbot, Devon

One of a very few malt-houses left in England using the traditional floor-malted method of production. This means that barley undergoing the malting process is turned regularly by hand. Originally opened in 1900, Tuckers supplies dozens of Westcountry breweries with high-quality malt, as well as others further afield. It is also the home of the SIBA South West Beer Festival every April. For those who want to learn more about the process of malting, regular daily tours are carried

Inside the germinating room at Tuckers Maltings, where germinating barley is turned by hand as seen here

out and there is a chance to sample the end result of malting at the conclusion of the tour with a pint from Teignworthy Brewery who share the building. A wonderful beer shop stocks a massive collection of bottled beers from all over the country. (See **Barley, Malt, Teignworthy.**)

Tuckers Maltings, Newton Abbot, one of the last surviving traditional maltings left in England and home to a wonderful bottled beer shop, seen on the bottom right of the photograph

V *is for*
vintage and a very spooky ale...

Vallance's   Sidmouth, Devon

Founded as the Sidmouth Brewery in 1832 by Richard Searle, it was renamed when brothers John and George Vallance took it over towards the end of the nineteenth century. Thirty-five pubs were owned and the brewery remained independent until 1946 when it was bought by London brewers Woodhead's. Brewing ended on the site in 1957 and it subsequently became a depot for Devenish until final closure in 1979.

Ventonwyn Brewery   Grampound Road, Cornwall

This eight-barrel plant was started by James Vincent in 1999, a year after his first brewery, Vincent's, closed. The name came from a nearby tin mine and apparently means 'white spring' in Cornish. The industrial theme continued throughout all the other beers, most of which were named after long-closed tin and copper mines in Cornwall. Beers produced were Old Pendenn (4%), Levant Gold (4%), Dolcoath Porter (4.6%) and a strong mild ale called Ding Dong (4.5%), as well as specials. The beers were well-received, with Gary Marshall at the Blisland Inn being one of the biggest fans. 'He brewed lots of different beers,' remembers Gary, 'golden ales, stouts, porters, and they were all good.' But the brewery closed in February 2001 and James Vincent is now working with cattle breeding. Even though he still enjoys his beer, he has no ambitions to go into brewing again. As for the Ventonwyn brewing kit and the name, this has been sold on and in the summer of 2002 a new Ventonwyn Brewery was getting ready to brew with former home-brewer Jack Wright at the helm. He is hoping to brew a 4.1% best bitter and no doubt further beers will follow. The brewery is now owned by Rolf Munding, who lives in Truro but also owns a brewery in Prague. Jack says:

He plans to rename the brewery The Wooden Hand or The Wooden Claw, so named after Sir John Carew Pole, who evidently lost a hand in a Civil War battle and had a replacement, made from wood, fitted in its place.

This original wooden hand is now owned (not worn) by a member of the family of Rolf's business partner.

(See **Vincent's**.)

Victoria Brewery   Mutley, Plymouth

Started brewing in the 1890s but was snapped up by Burton upon Trent brewers Samuel Allsopp at the end of the First World War. This was Allsopp's second purchase in Plymouth, the first being the Bedford Brewery the previous year. The two breweries were amalgamated under the name of New Victoria Brewery, but brewing finished in 1953. (See **Bedford Brewery**.)

Vincent's Brewery   Grampound, Cornwall

Postman and former soldier James Vincent had been brewing since he was thirteen when his home-brew won an award, as he told *What's Brewing* in 1999:

> *One of the three ales I entered in my first show was chosen best in Cornwall. I remember thinking if I could do this first time, what could I do next? I simply wanted to get to the stage where I could make a living as a brewer.*

Nearly twenty years later he had the chance when Vincent's was set up in the mid-1990s. It was a small-scale operation, given that he was still delivering the mail, but Spooky Ale, Aiden's Ale, named after his son, and Blisland 600 all had their fans. The beers were mainly found at the Blisland Inn. Disaster struck when the brewery burnt down in 1998, just as he was in the process of selling the plant and putting the money into a new one. This was followed a few months later by a motorcycle accident which laid him up for a few months. But by 1999 he was back in harness brewing again with Ventonwyn. (See **Ventonwyn**.)

Vintage Beers

It comes as a surprise to some people that beers can be laid down just like vintage bottles of wine. Generally speaking, beers that last have more alcohol in them than normal everyday drinking beer. Being bottle-conditioned also helps as the yeast in the bottle leads to a secondary fermentation. John Lawton at Teignworthy recommends that some of the Edwin Tucker beers he brews be left alone for some years so as to improve their character. Examples include the Empress Russian Porter and Victorian Stock Ale, which John thinks may keep for twenty to thirty years. Over the years, the taste of a vintage beer changes and develops, with hoppiness getting softer, maltiness more rounded and the complexity of the beer increasing.

W *is for*
white, winter and wheal ale...

Walter & Phillips   Totnes, Devon

Started brewing as Condy & Co at the Lion Brewery in the nineteenth century, before becoming Walter & Phillips. In 1899 it bought up neighbouring brewery William Sawyers and had an estate of 16 pubs. Operations came to an end in 1921 when the brewery and public houses went under the auctioneer's hammer.

Water

Brewers use water for cleaning their vessels and pipes, but they use liquor for making their beer. Both as you would guess are H_2O. Needless to say, good quality of water is essential for making good beer. In the nineteenth century brewers started to add various salts to their liquor so they could replicate the beers coming out of Burton upon Trent which had become incredibly popular. This was called Burtonisation and many brewers continue with this practice today – the main salts involved are gypsum (calcium sulphate) and Epsom salts (magnesium sulphate). (See **Brewing, Burtonisation**.)

Well

An important source of brewing liquor for a brewery before the days of mains water. These days few breweries have their own wells, partly because of pollution of the water table. Westcountry breweries getting their water from a well include O'Hanlon's and the Blue Anchor at Helston. There is a massive 'deep well' at St Austell which was apparently dug out by miners in the early-1900s. It was once used for brewing in the 1920s; today, however, it is occasionally used for general washing work.

Wheat Beer

When traditional cask-conditioned beer is brewed, the grist in the mash tun is usually pale malt, plus handfuls of crystal or coloured malt to add subtle variations in the flavour and colour. Wheat beers, on the other hand, are a mixture of pale and wheat malt, with the latter making up a sizeable percentage of the grist. This gives the beer a

St Austell's Clouded Yellow, an award winning wheat beer which has aromas of banana, crème brûlée and vanilla custard on the nose

zesty, tart and refreshing flavour while subtle hopping gives a lemony, spritzy fruitiness. In the last few years we have seen the popularity of wheat beers increase, as Bavarian and Belgian styles appear on the supermarket shelves. The Bavarian weiss beers feature banana, clove and vanilla flavour notes (this is the work of the yeast), while the Belgian ones tend to be spicy and almost peppery, thanks to the use of spices such as coriander seeds. British brewers have either tried to replicate these continental styles, or forged ahead with their own ale-tinged versions. Whatever the version, Westcountry wheat beers worth trying are the award-winning O'Hanlon's Wheat Beer (4%), Skinner's citrusy Cornish Blonde (5%) and St Austell's Clouded Yellow (5%).

Star Beer: St Austell, Clouded Yellow (5%) – Bavarian-style wheat beer from St Austell Brewery originally brewed as a one-off for the 1999 Celtic Beer Festival, which the brewery hosts annually. Vanilla pods, whole cloves and coriander seeds help to give the beer its refreshing and unique nose and palate. Think bananas, crème brûlée and bucketloads of vanilla custard for the nose, followed by clove and bananas on the palate and a dry, fruity finish. (See **St Austell**.)

Entrance to the Paradise Park where beer-loving birdwatchers look out for the Speckled Parrot

Wheal Ale Brewery   Hayle, Cornwall

Thirty years ago former Army officer Mike Reynolds set up the Paradise Bird Park at Hayle, which has since grown to become one of the most popular attractions in this far westerly part of Cornwall. Visitors come to see a stunning collection of rare birds, as well as otters and other animals. It is a great day out for the kids, as well as anyone who is ornithologically inclined. If you happen to be a real ale fan, then a double treat is in store, as the Bird in Hand, a solidly built former coaching house sitting next to the bird park, also brews its own ales. Founded in 1980 as the Paradise Brewery, it was one of a handful of small beer makers who kept the local beer drinkers happy in the years when the nationals had a stranglehold on the pubs in this area. Now known as Wheal Ale, former Navy aircraft engineer George Miller is at the helm as brewer. Along with his wife he also runs the pub which they lease from Paradise Park. Inside the Bird in Hand, the ceilings are high and hop sacks line the wall in part of the bar, while framed certificates attest their bar skills, brewing and best beer of the Cardiff Beer Festival in 1997.

*The Bird in Hand, Hayle, where hop sacks
line the walls and the odd Pickled Parrot
can occasionally be seen*

Until he arrived at the pub, George Miller, a native of South Shields,
had never brewed before. 'I always fancied running a pub when I came
out of the Navy,' he says, 'but I never thought I'd end up brewing.'
When he did start, George produced three beers, Paradise Bitter (3.8%),
Artists Ale (5.1%) and Victory (6%), which was only brewed at
Christmas. Things have changed over the years and there is only one
beer which is brewed all year round now: Speckled Parrot, a rich and
strong bitter which according to George came about through accident.
'It was a mistake but we kept the records of what we did and it is now
our best-selling real ale.' The other regular beer is Miller's, a golden
beer which is mainly produced for the summer. A hoppy and fruity
amber bitter, Golden Balls (4.3%), as the name suggests, was brewed for
the 2002 World Cup. In the winter, George Miller likes to experiment.
He says:

> *For the last three years in the winter we have produced trial-and-error
> beers. Last year we had Pickled Parrot (7.2%), a really dark beer. The year
> before we had Black Magic, which despite its name was not a stout.*

The brewery, a compact six-barrel plant, is situated at the back of the
pub in old stables, utilising old dairy equipment. George brews twice
a month, going up to three brews in the summer. He mills his own
malt, while his hops – Goldings and Fuggles – come from Kent. Yeast
is usually supplied by the Blue Anchor, a fellow brew-pub about 15
miles away. Even though it is a small operation, George Miller produces wonderful real ales, and his pub and brewery are a reminder of
the days when many such establishments made their own beer and got
on with the job in hand. And it seems to work. He points out an
elderly couple in the corner, revealing:

*Former Navy aircraft engineer George
Miller now fine-tunes beers instead of
engines at the Wheal Ale Brewery*

They are in their eighties. They come to the pub every day and have a Speckled Parrot and also take a couple of pints home with them.

Beers: Speckled Parrot (5.5%). Occasional: Miller's (4.3%), plus others. Bottles: Speckled Parrot, bottle-conditioned.
Star Beer: Speckled Parrot (5.5%) – Dark-brown in colour, with a rich nose of fruit cake, with hints of baked banana and citrus fruit. It is very malty on the palate, followed by citrus fruit, a hint of resiny hop and stewed fruit, before leading to a bitter and dryish finish which lingers. There is a slight sweetness and maltiness in the finish, adding up to a powerful and broad-flavoured strong ale which packs a punch. Certainly not a session ale, but two or three pints in the evening would leave you feeling very mellow.

White Ales

One of the best-known styles of beer in the nineteenth-century West Country (and allegedly beyond) were the so-called white ales of Kingsbridge, South Devon – 'the nappiest beer in all England,' according to one contemporary writer. These ales were apparently flavoured with eggs, milk and gin, plus a mysterious addition which was called 'grout'. They were supposed to be quite sweet and nutritious although some critics warned that white ales also contained pigeon droppings. The ales were certainly very thick, with the medical officer for Torquay describing them as looking 'like tea'. Drinkers tried to quaff the brew while leaving the sediment in the glass. White ales were not commercially brewed, but made on farms and in brew-pubs, with the recipe handed down. However, this did not stop a local rector from claiming a tithe on the white ales being produced. It was reputedly first brewed by a French doctor looking after French prisoners kept near Kingsbridge during the Napoleonic Wars. This style of beer was also produced in Newton Bushell, near Newton Abbot. It seemed to be on the way out in the latter decades of the nineteenth century, with the medical officer of Torquay (once again!) being recorded as saying in 1877 that white ales 'would soon be numbered as the things which had been'.

William Henry Mortimer   Kingskerswell, Devon

Small family brewery which was set up at the end of the nineteenth century. Kingskerswell is midway between Newton Abbot and Torquay, which would have been very handy for getting malt from Tuckers Maltings. Half a dozen local pubs were supplied until the brewery ceased trading in 1927.

Winter Ale

This strong, dark beer produced for the winter season is also called an old ale, strong ale, winter warmer and even Christmas beer. To make things even more confusing, there is a difference between the above beers and a barley wine, which is usually much stronger and varies in colour from dark to golden. Traditionally barley wine was also sold in small bottles called nips. Winter ales are traditionally dark, ranging from the blackness of stout to a solid chestnut-brown with reddish tinges. The nose can be incredibly complex with suggestions of stewed fruit, Christmas pudding, plus spices such as cinnamon, treacle, malt and toffee. In tasting they are full-bodied and often rich, with fruity, sweetish and occasionally subtle roast notes picked out on the palate. Any tendency towards an excess in sweetness is balanced by a generous amount of hops. The finish lingers like the warmth from a dying fire. They range in strength from 5% right up to 8%, though it is more usual to find them around the 6–7% mark. Westcountry examples include Blackawton's Winter Fuel (5%), Blue Anchor's Christmas Special (7.6%), Exe Valley's Winter Glow (6%) and the Beer Engine's Whistlemas (ABV varies between 6.3%–7.3%).

Star Beer: Blackawton Brewery, Winter Fuel (5%) – Reddish-brown winter ale which, as the name suggests, is one to take to combat the dampness of a Westcountry winter. On the nose there is a resiny and spicy hop with a fine balance of malt. On the palate flavours found include cough drops, Christmas spices and rich malt followed by a rounded hop fruitiness on the finish, with some caramel present. (See **Old Ale**.)

Add some spice to your seasonal drinking with Blackawton Brewery's Winter Fuel, which contains mace, aniseed and liquorice

X *is for* XXXX-stra strong...

XX

In the Middle Ages when a lot of brewing was done by monks, the familiar sign of the cross was used to denote various strengths; it was a guarantee of quality. When brewing companies such as Whitbread emerged in the seventeenth and eighteenth centuries, the sign was retained for marking the strength of beers. XX was mild ale (considered 'suitable for women'!), XXX a slightly stronger beer (suitable for men) and XXXX a strong beer. In the 1920s, St Austell's stock draught beers were XX, XXX and XXXX. Until recently St Austell named their malty, award-winning Mild XXXX (which despite the crosses was low in alcohol).

Y *is for* yeast and a yard of ale...

Yard of Ale

Nowadays we know it as a fun and messy way of drinking a beer in one go, but it is an old and venerable tradition. In 1685 the noted diarist John Evelyn makes a reference to a 'glasse of a yard long' in his diary, while legend has it that the three-foot-long thin glass with the bulb at the bottom was developed to meet the needs of stagecoach drivers who could drink without getting down or letting go of the reins. The Belgian strong ale Kwak is served in a scaled-down version of the yard-of-ale glass, held in a wooden bracket. This apparently was also developed with stagecoach drivers in mind. Nowadays, it can be seen at beer and folk festivals though not as much as in former years. Unwary drinkers can be surprised by modern yard-of-ale glasses where air collects in the bulb as the glass is lifted – this means that the final bit of beer can be forcefully splashed into the drinker's face.

Yeast

Single-cell fungus plant which converts malt sugars in the boiled hop wort into alcohol and carbon dioxide. Top-fermenting yeast is used for ales, with the yeast rising to the top of the fermenting beer and producing a large foamy head; bottom-fermenting yeast is used for lagers, with the yeast sinking to the bottom of the fermenting vessel and working in a lower temperature than its ale cousin. Before the mysteries of yeast were explained by Louis Pasteur and others, it was known as 'God-is-good' by brewers who turned to the Almighty when they could not work out how they ended up with such a potent brew. In many small breweries dried yeast is used with a fresh batch for each brew ('pitch and ditch', as one brewer called it), while others prefer to skim the yeast off the top of a brew and save it for the next one. A yeast that has been used for the same beer over a period of time, will have a specific character and adds its own particular imprint to the beer. (See **Brewing, Esters**.)

Fermenting vessel displaying traditional ridges in the head of yeast as it gets to work on the malt sugars to produce alcohol and carbon dioxide

Z is for
zzz...

Zymurgy

The last word on beer and brewing, meaning the study of fermentation in brewing.

Twelve of the Best
Some of the author's favourite Westcountry pubs

Blisland Inn   Blisland, Cornwall

The Blisland is a solidly built, slightly stern stone building dating from the end of the Victorian era. Inside the welcome is genuine and warm. The lounge bar has the feel of the old-fashioned parlour rooms you might remember glimpsing from childhood, with Toby jugs hanging from the dark wooden beams. Walk into the public bar and you are greeted by that most heart-warming sight: a row of handpumps dispensing ales both local and from further afield. Forthcoming beers are chalked up on a blackboard to whet the palate. Hundreds of pump-clips are tacked to the low wooden beams: so far landlord Gary Marshall has served nearly 2000 different real ales, and shows no sign of letting up. The Blisland Inn has been Cornwall CAMRA's pub of the year a couple of times, and was CAMRA's national pub of the year in 2001.

Above left: *Cornish pride: Blisland Inn, Blisland*
Above: *Inside the Blisland Inn, with landlord Gary behind the bar*

Blue Anchor   Helston, Cornwall

The Blue Anchor is the sort of place where people pop in for a quick one and emerge hours (or is it days?) later; time is an elastic concept here. Some people have been known to completely uproot their lives and move to Helston just so they can be near the pub which has been famous (or infamous) for its Spingo strong beers. Inside there are flag-stone floors which have been creased with generations of shoe leather; dark, grainy furniture and interiors; a small bar, and several drinking

Above: *The Blue Anchor*
Above right: *The 'locals' bar' at the Blue Anchor where time is elastic*

rooms off the corridor which runs from the front to the back, where the brewhouse can be found up a flight of stone stairs. A gem.

Boringdon Arms   Turnchapel, Plymouth, Devon

This is an imposing former quarrymaster's home, not far from Mount Batten, and a short ferry crossing from Plymouth. Inside there are two bars, with eight handpumps dispensing four regulars and four guest beers, usually from Westcountry brewers. There are also regular beer festivals. Inside it is cosy and atmospheric, while the food is excellent – the pies are particularly tempting! The local CAMRA branch has voted it pub of the year several times now, and rightly so.

Bridge Inn   Topsham, Devon

Several years back the Queen chose the Bridge for her first-ever visit to a pub – and what a choice. With its origins going back to the Middle Ages, the Bridge was a former brewhouse, and the old malt-house and brewery can still be seen behind the pub. Inside the pub is a warren of

The Bridge Inn, Topsham, which had the honour of being the first pub the Queen had ever visited

small old-fashioned rooms in which can be enjoyed a massive selection of real ales, mainly served from the barrel. This is the sort of pub where time stands still and before you know where you are, it is closing time.

Double Locks Hotel, Exeter: well worth a hike from Exeter

Double Locks Hotel   Alphington, Exeter

If you like a pint within sight of water, then this canal-side former lock-house from the eighteenth century is just the job. Even though technically Exeter lies to the front and the M5 to the back, the Double Locks feels like it is in the middle of the country. Once inside the simple, spacious unspoilt rooms you can enjoy an excellent selection of real ales served straight from the barrel. Good food too. Get there by following a lane from the Marsh Barton Trading Estate or hiking from the city along the historic Exeter canal which is about a mile or so. It is well worth the trek.

Duke of York   Iddesleigh, Devon

Thatch roof, piles of logs outside, uneven bedroom floors, log fires in the winter, beer straight from the barrel, good food and friendly bar staff; the Duke of York is one of those desert island pubs in which you would not mind being stranded. Dating back to the late Middle Ages, it is a long, low construction which was originally four cottages constructed for the chaps who built the nearby church. For somewhere so isolated and in such a small village, it gets busy very quickly which is a tribute to its award-winning licensees. Ted Hughes, the late Poet Laureate, was apparently a regular. The food is excellent, especially the breakfasts. A place to linger and, on clear days, enjoy the view of Dartmoor to the south-west.

Below left: Duke of York, Iddesleigh
Below: The bar at the Duke of York, Iddesleigh where beer is served straight from the barrel

Oxenham Arms   South Zeal, Devon

The first time I visited this ancient inn on the edge of Dartmoor there was thick fog everywhere, and the hunting horn and the hounds'

Above: *Oxenham Arms sign: a welcome sight in this small Dartmoor village*
Above right: *Oxenham Arms, South Zeal, where an ancient standing stone in the dining room is a reminder of the site's ancient past*

response could be heard eerily wafting through the mist. Inside the Oxenham all was warmth in the single cosy bar with a roaring log fire. Since then it has become a firm favourite. Beers are usually local, with Sharp's a regular. It is even more of a treat to stay there. Retire with your pint to a book-lined lounge and slumber in front of the monumental log fire. In the dining room there is an ancient standing stone which was incorporated into the fabric of the building.

Poltimore Arms   Yarde Down, Devon

Hidden away down lanes on the western edge of Exmoor, this old inn does not look much from outside. Enter and you are in an unspoilt and friendly moorland pub with a log fire in the main bar, whose exposed stone walls are decorated with antlers, hunting prints, old guns and farming implements. There are two further rooms, which share a woodburner, and have plenty of books for the beer-drinker who likes a browse. Beers (usually two, including Cotleigh Tawny), are served straight from the cask.

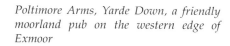

Poltimore Arms, Yarde Down, a friendly moorland pub on the western edge of Exmoor

Star Inn   Crowlas, Cornwall

The village of Crowlas can be found several miles outside Penzance, split in two by the busy A30. In the middle of the village stands the imposing red-brick Star Inn, which was formerly owned by Usher's and Courage. Nowadays, it is a no-frills, beer-drinker's pub run by former Cotleigh brewer Pete Elvin, whose dedication to the cause of real ale is reflected in the amount of pumpclips plastering the bar area. This is a pub where there are usually four to five beers on offer, coming from all corners of the British Isles. Pete also has plans to brew his own beer. A beer-lover's paradise.

*Below left: The Star Inn at Crowlas
Below: Landlord Pete Elvin and his stupendous collection of pumpclips which demonstrates his commitment to real ale*

Star Inn   St Just-in-Penwith, Cornwall

Former coaching inn built of rugged stone, moments from St Just's main square. Inside the single bar it is all dark wood with mementos of the town's association with seafaring and mining. The beers come from St Austell, served both by handpump and straight from the barrel. In an area where tourism has left its mark, this is a truly local pub with good beer and plenty of atmosphere. A few years back I spent a wonderful couple of rainy winter evenings here getting stuck into St Austell's sadly discontinued Winter Warmer.

The Great Western Hotel   Exeter, Devon

Every day is a beer festival at this traditional railway hotel, a stone's throw from St David's Station. The bar usually has 12 real ales on, a mixture of Westcountry and interesting ones from further up North, plus regulars from Exe Valley and Suffolk brewers Adnams. It is a lively, bustling place most of the day and a good place to start and finish an Exeter pub crawl.

Thistle Park Brewhouse   Plymouth, Devon

Standing on the corner of a busy crossroads, this old Victorian pub is home to Sutton Brewery, so you will always get a chance of tasting their excellent beers. Inside the pub it is an unfussy bare-wood-and-pews interior. There is music some nights and in recognition of landlord Quintin Style's South African background, the dried and salted meat biltong as well as boerewors sausages are also sold. A wonderful city pub in which to while away a Saturday afternoon with the papers.

Thistle Park Brewhouse, an ideal place to study the complexities of Sutton Brewery's magnificent beers

Bibliography

Baillie, Frank *The Beer Drinker's Companion.* David & Charles, 1973

Baker, Julian L *The Brewing Industry.* Methuen & Co, 1905

Barber, Norman *A Century of British Brewers 1890–1990.* A Brewery History Society Publication, 1994

Barber, Sally & Chips *Haunted Pubs in Devon.* Obelisk Publications, 1995

Boston, Richard *Beer And Skittles.* Collins, 1976

Denham, Chris *The Local.* Denham Books, 1999

Evans, Jeff *Good Bottled Beer Guide.* CAMRA, 2001

Gates, Brian *Tuckers Maltings 1900-2000: History in the Making*

Glover, Brian *CAMRA Dictionary of Beer.* Longman, 1985

Gregory, Conal & Knock, Warren *Beers of Britain.* Cassell, 1975

Haydon, Peter *The English Pub: A History.* Hale, 1994

Jackson, Michael *Beer Companion.* Mitchell Beazley, 1997

James, Edward *The Best Beers and Ciders of South West England* Broadcast Books, 1994

Jones, Michael *Time, Gentlemen, Please! Early Brewery Posters in the Public Record Office.* Pro Publications, 1997

Luck, Liz *Brewing For Cornwall; The Story of St Austell Brewery 1851–2001.* St Austell, 2001

Madgin, Hugh *Best of British Bottled Beer.* Dial House, 1995

Miles, Mary *Hancock's Brewery Wiveliscombe.* Somerset Industrial Archaeological Society, 1985

Pepper, Barrie *The Bedside Book Of Beer* Alma Books, 1990

Peaty, Ian P *You Brew Good Ale: A History of Small-scale Brewing.* Sutton, 1997

Protz, Roger *The Taste Of Beer.* Weidenfeld & Nicholson, 1998

Protz, Roger *Classic Stout & Porter.* Prion, 1997

Protz, Roger *The Real Ale Almanac.* NWP/CAMRA, 1999

Protz, Roger & Sykes, Homer *The Village Pub* Weidenfeld & Nicholson, 1992

Titcombe, Graham & Andrews, Nicolas *The Guest Beer Guide '97.* Foulsham, 1997

Trevail, B *Curious Cornwall.* Tor Mark Press, 1969

Webb, Anne (editor) *Dictionary Of Beer.* CAMRA, 2001

Webb, Tim *The Best Pubs In Devon & Cornwall.* Alma Books, 1989
Wyatt, Monica *Historic Inns of Devon.* Bossiney Books, 1986
Young, Jimmy *A Short History of Ale.* David & Charles, 1979

Other information came from the free newsletters that are produced by CAMRA branches, including One & Ale (Cornwall CAMRA); Exe Ale (Exeter & East Devon CAMRA); Beer'tiz (North Devon CAMRA).

Word For Word: An Encyclopaedia of Beer. Whitbread & Co, 1953
Inns & Outs. A Devon Life Publication 2001
Moor To Sea: The Devon Real Ale Guide CAMRA, 1993
Real Ale In Cornwall CAMRA, 1987
Real Ale In Cornwall CAMRA, 2002
Real Ale In Devon CAMRA, 1981
The Devon Real Ale Guide CAMRA, 1990
Devon Real Ale CAMRA, 1987
Good Beer Guide CAMRA, various editions
Real Ale In Cornwall CAMRA, 1986
The Hop Guide: A Guide to the Culture, Production and Use of Hops in England